Commendations for

GUINEA PIG FOR LUNCH

'I've never tasted guinea pig but can all too easily imagine it! Having shared in one of Stephen's 'intrepid journeys', I've been able to re-live some of the bizarre encounters and moving situations which I've so valued during my long relationship with Tearfund.

Thanks, Stephen, for your memory for detail which I'd long forgotten, for your dry humour, and for renewing the challenges which confront us from a desperately needy world.'

Sir Cliff Richard

'Sparkles with life and interest, a very good read indeed.'

Adrian Plass

'Reading this made me laugh and cry – a window on corners of the world where hardship and poverty are met by courage, enterprise, and the most humble faith. A book to challenge, inspire – and entertain!'

Pam Rhodes

'An absorbing read. Stephen Rand combines the highs and lows of international travel with profound insights into the lives of the people he meets at each journey's end.'

Jill Dando

'Under the cover of a host of good stories important principles of mission and faith abound.'

Stephen Gaukroger

The author and publishers are grateful to the following for permission to quote:

Quote from 'Ballad of a Thin Man' by Bob Dylan, reproduced from *Bob Dylan – Writings and Drawings*, Panther 1974

Quotes from 'Broken Image' and 'The Road to Freedom' by Garth Hewitt, © Chain of Love Music

Quotes from 'To Feel your Compassion' and 'Beauty for Brokenness' by Graham Kendrick, © Make Way Music

Quote from 'Cathedral' in *Homeland* by Stewart Henderson, Hodder & Stoughton 1993

Quote from 'This is your Land' by Simple Minds, © EMI Virgin Music Ltd

Quote from 'The Road to Hell' by Chris Rea, © Posedrive Ltd 1990, reproduced by permission of IMP Ltd

Quotes from 'Love Never Gives Up', 'Bulange Downpour' and 'There's no Power in Pity' by Sir Cliff Richard, reproduced courtesy of Patch Music

Quote from 'Precious' by Martyn Joseph, © EMI Music

GUINEA PIG FOR LUNCH

THE EXPERIENCES OF AN INTREPID WORLD TRAVELLER

STEPHEN RAND

Fellowship around the guinea pig —
a lifetime of friendship!
All the best
Stephen

Hodder & Stoughton
LONDON SYDNEY AUCKLAND

First published in Great Britain in 1998

The right of Stephen Rand to be identified as the Author of
the Work has been asserted by him in accordance with
the Copyright, Designs and Patents Act 1988.

Cover photographs by Richard Hanson and Mike Webb of Tearfund

10 9 8 7 6 5 4 3

British Library Cataloguing in Publication Data
A record for this book is available from the British Library

ISBN 0 340 72158 8

Typeset by Avon Dataset Ltd, Bidford-on-Avon, Warks

Printed and bound in Great Britain by
Clays Ltd, St Ives plc

Hodder and Stoughton Ltd
A Division of Hodder Headline PLC
338 Euston Road
London NW1 3BH

for Susan
your support and encouragement has meant everything to me

– to Katharine and Helen, who have grown up without showing any apparent emotional scars from my absences or the naff T-shirts I gave them on my returns; thanks for always, along with your mother, making sure I was glad to come home.

– to my father, for setting me on the right road, and continuing to give me an example of faithful service and gentlemanly godliness.

– to Tearfund, for offering a channel for me to express those things that mattered most to me, and allowing my spare-time activity to become my full-time employment: it is a rare privilege to earn a living doing something so close to one's heart; I am deeply grateful, too, for the opportunity to travel and for the time to write this book about my discoveries and experiences, especially as I am acutely aware of those of my colleagues whose travels have been far more meaningful and intrepid than mine.

– to all my travelling companions, those named and not named in this book: special thanks for being such good company, for allowing friendship to develop, and for coping with my snoring, my irritations, my itineraries, my conversation and even occasionally my sermons; my travels would not have been the same without you.

– to all my hosts, Tearfund partners who have given their time and themselves for the sake of my understanding: thank you for every demonstration that the word is still becoming flesh and living among us; for enabling me to experience a little of the worst the world has to offer in the company of some of the best.

Contents

Preface

The disease

You have just returned from the travel experience of a lifetime – or perhaps no more than a weekend in Blackpool. You might even have just come home after four years in a remote corner of deepest Africa. You have so many stories to tell, so many impressions to share, so many photographs to show.

You are desperate for someone to listen, to be interested, to share and reflect your enthusiasm. And can you find them? So many seem indifferent. They must be too busy, too self-centred; perhaps they are just jealous. Then the paranoia sets in. Is the truth that you are a travel bore, your slide and video shows renowned as something to avoid at all costs?

Rejection can be painful. The lack of interest can be crushing, the glazed look completely dispiriting. Somehow your whole experience has been lessened, reduced, because there is no one to tell about it, no one wants to know.

The cure

I have discovered the cure for this holiday illness, this stomach-churning travel tummy. It is simple: write a book.

You can tell every story, recall every anecdote. You can describe the funny episode, the repulsive meal, the primitive sanitation, the extraordinary characters, the moving moment, the exotic location, the desperate journey – all human life is there, and you don't have to leave anything out.

Because you won't be there when (if?) anyone reads it, you don't have to experience the rejection, the lack of interest or the glazed look. In fact, you may even convince yourself that everyone else will find the book just as interesting and exciting as you did – and still do. It's a long-term, hard-work therapy, it has several potentially damaging side-effects. But it's effective. You can at last share your experience with your friends and relatives – and they have to thank you for the present.

Tearfund has sent me to remote, exotic, interesting places and people so that I could write and talk about them when I came back. I have dared to write this book because some people who have heard me speak, read my articles and seen my videos have responded: some with laughter, a few with tears, enough with appreciation to make this particular therapy seem a worthwhile exercise.

Inevitably my experiences are a series of snapshots, frozen in time. They are vivid, they are real, they are reported as accurately as possible, they are also dated. Some go back nearly twenty years. Places will have changed. Tearfund's partners will have changed, both their people and their work – they may even no longer be Tearfund partners. Tearfund has changed, and I have changed. I have reported as I found, and what I found has changed me. Thank God, who does not change, that change is his family business. That's good news to the poor.

1

In at the Deep End

Because something is happening here
But you don't know what it is
Do you, Mister Jones?

Bob Dylan

Aeroplanes are wonderful. Aeroplanes are mysterious. And aeroplanes are weird. They are wonderful because they can transport you to other worlds in hours. They are mysterious because they stay in the air when common sense tells you it is impossible. They are weird because they are flying tubes of Western civilisation, enclosed and suspended six miles up in the sky with enough fuel, food, water and consumer culture on board – just enough to reach the destination without running out.

Every flight is a wonderfully weird game of 'Let's pretend'. Let's pretend I am one of the jet-set rich being pampered in a luxury world of comfort, even though a sardine in a tin might have slightly more leg-room. Let's pretend I am having an exotic gourmet meal, whereas in fact I am trying to work out how they design, produce and package the meal while attempting to unwrap the knife and fork and then eat the dainty morsels without fatally wounding my neighbour with my elbows.

On that first flight to India, it was also let's pretend I am a young but mature business executive, quite used to air transport, seeing it as no more than a convenient way to travel a long distance in a short time. Let's pretend that there is nothing exciting about free drinks, a free film, the comedy channel on the headphones. Let's pretend I am an adult who can take this or leave it. Don't let anyone guess that I am as excited about the flight as I am apprehensive about the second adventure that is due to start where the first one ends – at Bombay airport.

But when the drinks have been drunk, the film has been watched, the old jokes laughed at, the meal eaten, the flight still only seems to have just begun. Half-dozing, thinking about what should have been done before I left, and what should be done when I arrive. Before my mind is broadened for ever, perhaps I should reflect on the journey that has led up to this potentially life-changing experience . . .

I sold my drum-kit to buy the engagement ring. I was married at twenty-one, far too young, my mother said. We honeymooned in Corfu. For Susan and me, this was our first trip in an aeroplane. It was memorable, if only because it ended with a dramatic view of a plane that had finished an earlier flight half on the runway and half in the water. This was neither the best nor even the main memory of our honeymoon, neither did it set the tone for our whole marriage as a brush with disaster, but as I settled into the life of a history teacher I do remember wondering if I would ever fly again.

I had been a revolting student; my desire to change the world rarely became anything as energetic as action, preferring radical contempt and intellectual criticism to dirty hands and serious inconvenience. I squatted and marched – but only once each. I was one of the Sidney Sussex Seven, facing a full disciplinary hearing for my student activism. I was fined £4, then let off on appeal. Now I was teaching students, not so much revolting as challenging. Daily survival depended on a combination of dramatic performance, rapid thinking and an outer shell of apparent confidence, all of which were usually effective if occasionally exhausting and draining. Sometimes I even added lesson preparation as a novel ingredient.

Revolting student and regular churchgoer were certainly conflicting images. At university I hung on to my faith – or perhaps it was God who decided to hang on to me. My tutor commented that he had never known a student finish the three years with the same girlfriend as he had started with. I was glad to give him an exception to that particular rule, and he was probably just as surprised that I finished three years with the same faith as well. It was a close-run thing.

One problem was that I was convinced that non-Christians, with no religious or moral scruples to hold them back, must be having more fun. But it didn't take long to discover that they were often pretty miserable. Sex, drugs and drink didn't really seem to do it for them. I particularly liked one friend's complaint that he had to drink several pints to feel as happy for a few minutes as I appeared to be all the time, even without the benefit of alcohol.

The church was the other problem. Middle-class, middle-aged, conservative, thoughtless, uncaring – changing the world did not seem to be on the agenda. A significant part of this rage focused on to the slightly irrational contrast of church as a prelude to Sunday lunch in a world of a billion starving people. I sat in the balcony looking down literally and metaphorically on those who seemed to have found a faith that allowed such comfortable complacency. I nearly got lost in the gap between the church and the real world.

Susan was a social worker rather than a student. As a result she was sensible, knew far more about the real world than I did, and she kept my feet on the ground. When we were married I became her personal case-load of one. But the rage was still there and the gap still concerned me. Then I discovered Tearfund. Tearfund built a bridge and gave me a lifeline: there were real Christians around who wanted to change the world. And they didn't just talk about it!

I can't remember exactly how we first discovered Tearfund's Tearcraft catalogue. But it certainly changed our lives. It was full of handmade craft items made by needy people who would otherwise be without employment. I thought that being able to buy Christmas presents that also helped the people who had made them was such a brilliant idea that I took the catalogue into the staff-room, and passed it round to collect orders. They seemed to like it too, and I ended up with quite a big order – over £200. This was the 1970s, remember – that was more than I earned in a month.

Tearcraft must have thought it was a big order, too, because they wrote and asked us if we would consider becoming voluntary sales representatives. We obviously missed the government health warning, because we said yes, and embarked on a career of spare-time Tupperware and jumble sale-style retailing that took us all over London, from our own front-room (when no one turned up) almost via Figges Marsh to the Royal Albert Hall. We tried not to be sick of sikas or to bungle the ordering of bangles. We marvelled at the miah man, a ju-ju-like jute doll that was surely unsellable – until someone actually bought it.

Surviving in London on a teacher's salary was not easy, let alone giving a lot to charity. But selling Tearcraft was providing employment to the poor in the Third World, enabling us to make money to give back to Tearfund, and giving me the opportunity to remind some of those seemingly lost in complacent Christianity of the real world outside. Our turnover grew to several thousand pounds a year. We made friends – Bob and Mary Groves, Lynda and Jeremy Page, were Tearcraft reps who moved into West Norwood, worked with us and became some of our closest friends. We got to know some of the Tearcraft staff, and found our front-room focus Haitian wall-carving in a dusty corner of the Newcastle warehouse. It was great. It was even more fun than marking essays. One member of the nation of shopkeepers had found his niche.

One year we came back from a summer holiday and among the letters, bills and junk on the mat was a copy of *Third Way* magazine. In the situations vacant column was a job advert from Tearfund. They were looking for someone to develop the representatives network. It was almost as if I had written the job description for myself. I applied. I was invited for an interview. Susan and I drove over to Teddington, parked by the river and were joined by a one-legged pigeon as we talked over the possibilities and the implications. I was interviewed, and eventually I was offered the job.

I started on the first working day of 1979. The Tearfund office in Station Road Teddington was reopening after refurbishment, so I arrived to be shown to a room with no desk, no chair, no telephone. It was completely bare. The uncertain mix of positive and negative signals this created was reinforced by the news that the day before I started had been the last day for the person who had interviewed me. Was his decision to leave a vote of confidence in the new appointment, a washing of the hands or desperation to escape before I arrived? Or could it, possibly, have had nothing to do with me at all?

Tearfund policy was that new employees should not make a visit overseas until they had been at work for at least a year. So I travelled the length and breadth of the British Isles, encouraging (hopefully) the existing voluntary reps, meeting and appointing new ones, beginning to build a team of regional staff and taking meetings. Taking meetings meant telling people about the wonderful job Tearfund was doing . . . and after a year I was now about to discover the truth for myself.

Just before I boarded the plane, George Hoffman, the visionary who had already turned a good idea into a major UK charity without a single flag day or door-to-door collection, who set guiding principles for Tearfund and for my own communication that still apply today, called me into his office. I waited to hear the words of spiritual insight and wisdom that would inspire and inform my journey into the unknown. He was terse and to the point. 'Whatever you do,' he said, 'don't drink anything which isn't bottled or boiled.'

The plane landed at Bombay. We negotiated the curious limbo of bland concrete that is arrival halls the world over, all apparently designed to give the impression that you could be anywhere rather than somewhere. I was travelling with Frank Thompson, a warm-hearted Irishman and one of Tearfund's older staff, who had brought his business experience to bear on the challenge of managing Tearcraft after its founder, Richard Adams, had left and established a confusingly similar business called Traidcraft.

Frank was on a trip to visit existing and possible new Tearcraft producers, collecting samples of potential new products and placing orders for the next mail-order catalogue. He was the first of many colleagues I got to know as a result of travelling together, and I was glad of his experience that first night.

Nothing had, or perhaps could have, prepared me for the impact of my first minutes of experience of the Third World. I stepped through the door of the arrivals hall into another world. The first thing that hit me was the heat. It was now about midnight, it was January, it was dark . . . and it was hot. I think the hall must have been air-conditioned, because it was like stepping out into an open-air sauna. It seemed unnatural.

And then there were the people. It was midnight, it was January, it was dark . . . and there were people everywhere. There were children, there were beggars, there were policemen, there were street-sellers, there were passengers who knew what they were doing, rushing off into the night. There were also the taxi-drivers. They spotted us. Their touts spotted us. We were potential customers.

Actually we weren't potential customers. Because Frank knew where we were staying and Frank knew the hotel had a courtesy bus. Frank knew that this bus would come to the point where we were standing and pick us up. He knew this even when the bus came towards us and then drove past, ignoring his vigorous signals. He knew this even when ten minutes later the bus came towards us again, and drove past us again, ignoring his even more vigorous signals. He kept to his beliefs when another ten minutes passed, and so did another bus.

Impressed as I was by a man who keeps his faith in the face of discouragement, who perseveres in spite of hardship, who believes despite all evidence to the contrary, I was also aware of growing numbers of taxi touts who were convinced we were about to become the geese who might lay golden eggs. They cajoled, they pleaded, they laughed (what did they know that we didn't, I wondered?), they might even have threatened. I certainly felt threatened.

I felt threatened because of the uncertainty, the unfamiliarity. I just did not know what to do next. I was not in control. It was dark, it was hot, it was noisy. I was the odd one out. It was not my world. It was exciting, yes, but slightly scary. Everyone else knew what was going on, but I did not. I had stepped into another world.

Eventually the hotel bus did stop, Frank's confidence finally vindicated. It was a posh hotel too, its marble halls adding another bizarre quirk into the whirling kaleidoscope of the first twenty-four hours of my first overseas visit. I began to discover a common feature of my travels: the way time suddenly becomes elongated. Each section of a journey seems like a whole day; so much varied and unusual experience is packed into a few hours that they appear to have lasted much longer. One day seems like three, three days a week. After ten days I am convinced I have been away for a month.

The first hour the next day was another immersion in the Third World maelstrom. It began with an unforgettable taxi ride. *Your Life in Their Hands* was the title of a TV series about surgeons at work. At least their patients were anaesthetised. Being driven in India is like being given a guided tour of a real-life Indiana Jones movie. I have never bothered with the white-knuckle rides at theme parks; I have been in a Bombay taxi. Premila Pavamani in Calcutta would one day explain to me that she prayed every time her husband Vijayan went out in the car.

I was reminded of this when he was driving down one of the widest and grandest streets in Calcutta. We pulled out to overtake the car that was overtaking the bus that was overtaking the lorry that was overtaking the bicycle that was overtaking the bicycle rickshaw that was overtaking the hand-drawn rickshaw that was manoeuvring round the sacred cow that was forcing a pedestrian into the gutter. We ended up pulling further and further out, until we were forcing a car coming in the opposite direction almost off the road. As we passed there was a line of ten abreast – nine going one way, one the other.

But the traffic, and the driving, was only part of the experience. What I recall most from that day was that it was worst when we stopped. Because it seemed that at every traffic light there was a beggar waiting. It was hot, and survival in the taxi meant having the window open. Survival for the beggars meant spotting the white face and the open window. Small girls carrying tiny babies, hands outstretched into the car. The eyes were sad, pleading. Except for one. Suddenly, as we waited at one traffic light, a head thrust itself into my line of vision. The empty eye sockets of an old blind man were no more than two feet away. I could see, but I did not know where to look. I had not even got any Indian money. I prayed for the lights to change. When they had, I was left sweating, ashamed, confused.

Eventually we arrived. Frank was visiting the office of a Tearcraft partner to discuss orders. After introductions had been made, I was given permission to venture outside, carrying my Super 8 cine camera. Perhaps some film of the traffic would liven up those midweek church missionary meeting slide shows.

The office was in an upmarket downtown area, not far from the Sheraton Hotel. Just across the road another five-star luxury hotel was being built. The marble reception area was already taking shape. But what caught the eye was the builders and the building process.

The scaffolding was not the rigid strength of steel, but the spindly spider's web of bamboo stalks lashed together, uncertainly weaving their way up the sides of the twenty-storey building. In place of hoists and lifts they had ramps steeply zigzagging their way up. As I watched the men pushing wheelbarrows of cement up and up, I realised the phrase 'cheap labour' meant real people sweating out real work for very little real money. Ever since, I have tried to avoid the phrase 'abject poverty'. I have seen people working, labouring, sweating, toiling. I have rarely seen people abject.

At the foot of the hotel, part of the building site, was a mini-shantytown. I could see women and children alongside their pitiful homes, which were little more than rudimentary tents made from jute sacking and bits of wood. I focused the camera on one particular child, then got arty and attempted a slow zoom in on the child that would start with the posh hotel, take in the shanty camp-site and show just who lived there. As the child slowly filled the viewfinder I suddenly realised that I had caught him in the act of defecating. Perhaps not so suitable for that midweek meeting.

As I took in the reality of the whole scene, I worked out that presumably the workmen came and lived on the building site with their families. No point in building anything too elaborate for themselves. When the hotel was ready for its £100-a-night guests, those who had earned perhaps less than £100 a year building it would move on. Months later I was reading a passage from Isaiah 65, describing how the Messiah will come and change the world; it was as though a light clicked on, and I suddenly realised that the Bible connected into the Third World experience in a special way: *'They will build houses and dwell in them . . . no longer will they build houses and others live in them.'*

That evening I spent some time with the people who ran the handicraft business based in Bombay, the people Frank had come to see. They were the first Christians from outside my own culture I had ever met. One of my hesitations before I left had been that having spent a year talking about the way Tearfund worked with evangelical Christian partners, I could not help wondering what exactly they would be like. Would their Christianity be quite the same as mine? Would I discover that the cultural gap was such that it prevented real fellowship?

There were four or five of them, Indian men and women. We had a pleasant meal together and the conversation flowed. Suddenly one topic gripped them fiercely. It was debated hard, the temperature rose – this one really mattered. Should a Christian charity accept money from non-Christians? As the discussion ranged from biblical text to anecdote to opinion and back to biblical text I listened with interest. The question hardly seemed to merit such passion, but I felt at home; this was a Christianity I knew. Then I realised why. These business people were middle class, and all members of the Christian Brethren, the very same denomination I had grown up in. I had travelled thousands of miles, and the first Christians I met matched my Christianity not just vaguely, but right down to the smallest sub-section of the evangelical sub-culture. Who says God has no sense of humour?

2

The Overnight Train

If God had intended us to fly,
he never would have given us the railways.
                                        Flanders and Swann

Bangladesh was the home of Tearcraft. After the cyclone disaster
that had so closely followed the civil war that led to the birth of
the nation, Tearfund had arranged for a plane-load of relief
supplies to be sent. George Hoffman then had a brain-wave: why
not find a way to make the return flight of benefit to the suffering
people of Bangladesh? So the plane was filled with handicrafts,
purchased from producers who if they had known about Christmas
would have thought it must have come early. A catalogue was
produced to sell these craft goods to Tearfund supporters, and
Tearcraft was born.

Bangladesh dominated its infancy as well. Susan and I became
familiar with the unmistakable aroma of Bangladeshi jute as we
opened the boxes when our orders arrived. Sikas were the key
product, and sikas were the making of Tearcraft. Fashionable
1970s interior design demanded a hanging basket; what better to
hang one in than an attractive ethnic subtle reworking of a brown-
string bag, available in myriad shapes and sizes, to suit every
domestic location? Not only did Susan and I sell thousands of
them; we also untangled thousands of them. When I began to
travel round the country to visit Tearfund representatives, I always

11

knew I was at the right house by the Tearcraft sika hanging in the porch.

Frank and I travelled on together to Bangladesh, where I was to discover that the sika and basket were simply a practical everyday storage method in homes that struggled for shelves, let alone cupboards or even pantries: they kept the contents off the floor and away from rats. We flew into Dhaka late one evening on a crowded Bangladesh Biman plane that I remember with affection only for its in-flight catering – a chicken curry sandwich delivered to each seat in a greaseproof paper bag. It landed late, and when we eventually cleared customs we were met by Geoff Evans, a Tearfund worker helping HEED (Health, Education and Economic Development) Bangladesh with the business side of their craft operation.

He was Irish, so the fact that the overnight train I was supposed to be catching was now due to have left the station made him neither agitated nor irritated. This was just a challenge to be met with optimism, enthusiasm . . . and manic driving. The darkness only added to the thrill of the chase. Taxis, buses, rickshaws – all were scattered, swerved round and just about avoided as we dashed from airport to station, hoping that Bangladesh Railways' reputation for erratic inefficiency was entirely accurate and deserved.

As Geoff hurtled the car round the Dhaka obstacle course, he explained that if the train was still there he would show me the carriage where my seat was booked, and where I would find the Browns, Tearfund personnel on their way to the same destination, who would look after me and make sure I got off at the right place. He would be staying in Dhaka to discuss business with Frank, but I would be fine . . . 'No problem.'

We screeched to a halt at the station entrance. The train was there. I grabbed my suitcase, said goodbye to Frank, who was sitting in the back of the car and looking a little green of face. I lumbered (the suitcase was heavy, and so was I) across the concourse and on to the platform. Geoff was ahead clutching my ticket. At that moment the train decided that an hour late was quite enough, and began to move. The platform was low, the carriage floor was a few feet higher. Geoff leapt on to the nearest step, hauled me and my suitcase on board, said something very rapidly to the Bangladeshi carriage attendant, pushed my ticket into my hand and jumped off. He ran alongside the train for a few metres, shouted, 'Have a nice trip!' and then disappeared into the darkness.

I looked at the attendant. He looked at me. The full extent of my predicament began to dawn. He spoke no English and my Bengali was remarkably rusty. Neither of us seemed to know where my bunk in the sleeping compartment might be. I knew I was due to arrive in Kamalganj at around 5.00 a.m. (if the train was running to time) but as I looked out of the window I realised another complication. As the end of the platform disappeared from view, I caught a glimpse of what I assumed to be the station sign. If it said Dhaka it certainly did not say it in any letters I could read. Perhaps Bengali would have been a more useful school option than Latin.

Before I could get depressed by the situation, the train slowed and came to a halt. There scarcely seemed to have been a gap between the end of the Dhaka platform and the start of this new one. Suddenly I became aware that I was being shouted at. A white face was peering up at me out of the darkness; Stephen Brown had come looking for me, alerted by Geoff to my arrival. Once again I grabbed my suitcase for another lumber up the platform. It was obviously a long train, and the scramble seemed to go on for ever. But eventually a finger pointed at my carriage, just as the train began to move again. For the second time in ten minutes I was jumping on to a moving train.

I had found my compartment. I had found my bunk. I had found the Browns. And I had found their luggage. Mounds of it. They had been down to Dhaka to collect their sea freight, all the belongings they had packed weeks ago in Britain. Now boxes, cases and barrels were packed into the compartment. I didn't care. I was pleased to see them, and know there was someone who would be able to read the station sign.

I was sort of dozing when someone said, 'Kamalganj'. The plans had been made. The train did not wait until everyone had disembarked before restarting, apparently. It just stopped, waited for an undefined length of time, then started again. So time was of the essence. The shipload had to be unloaded as rapidly as possible. Watches had been synchronised and tasks assigned. I had my orders. The carriage window was lowered, the Browns leapt out of the door. My job was to pass the luggage out of the window to them on the platform, preferably without dropping it on to either them or the platform, which seemed even lower than it had in Dhaka. Suitcase followed box followed barrel. As I handed the last one out of the window, the train lurched into movement. I ran down the corridor and leapt the few feet on to the platform. I had arrived in Kamalganj.

I had an enjoyable few days in rural Bangladesh. My epic train journey gave me some very slight status, perhaps only curiosity value, among the expats. I was shown round by Tearfund's Ann Burt, a physiotherapist, and Chris Smith. Tearfund's Overseas Personnel scheme had also started in Bangladesh, just as Tearcraft had. Chris had been one of the original group of nurses who arrived to help care for the victims of civil war and cyclone, and now she had become part of HEED, a consortium of Christian missions and aid agencies established to encourage co-operation and effectiveness in meeting the desperate needs of the people.

At Kamalganj HEED had taken over a leprosy hospital that had been built but never used. Now, because of Christian concern and initiative, it was the base not only for leprosy treatment, but also for community healthcare and handicrafts. Chris drove me over, and occasionally round, the concrete bridges that were an interesting part of the dusty tracks. The four-wheel drive Land Rover demonstrated its versatility as we visited surrounding villages where HEED was involved. Particularly memorable was visiting the Manipuri back-strap weavers, tribal people demonstrating traditional skills, long swathes of beautifully coloured cloth stretched from the simple loom fastened round the weaver's back up to the eaves of their immaculately simple dried mud houses.

It was in Kamalganj that I was introduced to the idea of fish-farming. Tearfund worker Bob Hansford explained just how fast tilapia could grow, how many could be grown in a typical sized pond and just how healthy fish could be as part of the local diet. I was particularly impressed by the cow-dung floating in the middle of the pond, which was apparently there to feed the fish. And no doubt it improved their flavour.

This theme returned as Chris was taking me past another pond on the edge of a village. There were cows standing (and doing more than standing) on the far side. Closer to us there was a rich green slime covering the water. Chris casually commented that HEED had provided a tube well in the village, providing a plentiful supply of healthy clean water. But the people, she said, still preferred the pond water: it tasted better.

When I tell this story in schools I can almost see the faces revealing just how stupid they think these people must be. Even explaining that we only know about germs because we have been told about them by teachers and television ads does not help much. Neither does pointing out the logic of their position: they had drunk the water all their lives, so clearly the water could not be dangerous, something else must be killing so many of their children. But when I ask the pupils how many of them smoke, and some own up, I am able to demonstrate that we are just as capable of opting for taste over health, against all the evidence.

GUINEA PIG FOR LUNCH

* * *

Sunday morning. We went to church; a small group gathered, including some of the leprosy patients, and Stephen Brown preached on Jesus and leprosy, it being World Leprosy Sunday. It seemed extraordinary that, two thousand years on, this topic was still so vitally relevant. Some of these people had been thrown out of their homes; they knew what it meant to be thought 'unclean'; they understood the significance of a Saviour who would reach out and touch the leper.

Now treatment was available and effective. I had sat alongside a group who also sat with their feet immersed in a bowl of water. Keeping the skin soft and supple was vital, a lesson they had learned because some Christians still cared enough to open, staff and run the leprosy hospital that would otherwise have remained an empty shell of unfulfilled hope.

After the service, the relevance of the link to the life and times of Jesus was reinforced in a viciously painful way. It started innocently and exotically enough; my hosts were keen to give me a satisfactory Sunday lunch, and took me down to the local market to get some meat. We approached a table at the end of the market. There was nothing on the table, just a scrawny awning flapping lazily over one end of the table, and an equally scrawny goat tied by its ankle to one leg of the table.

Something was said to the man behind the table. Uncomprehendingly I watched him untie the goat and lead it behind a piece of canvas a few metres away. A minute later he emerged and handed over a plastic bag. It was only when my host announced that he now had what was needed for lunch that comprehension dawned. To a man used to the idea that Sunday joints come shrink-wrapped in a choice of sizes, it was a brutal reminder of why butchers are called butchers. In Bangladesh, the wealthy meat-eater's choice was deciding which of the four legs looked the most appetising.

Our attendance at the market had been noticed. As we had

walked towards the butcher's table, I was confronted by a beggar, his voice beseeching, his hand out-thrust. I recognised, in a kind of suspended horror, that he must know something about butchery, because he simply had no legs. I hardly took it in. To everyone else he was just a part of the scene; but no one had prepared me for this, I had no established pattern of response to fall back on.

I can't remember now whether I had any cash with me. I think I must have done, but being naturally mean, and having no idea of the protocol, and never having done it before, I managed to close my heart and my purse. In India that first beggar had disappeared when the traffic lights changed; in the Bangladeshi market-place there was to be no such swift escape. As I walked past him, he called out again. I walked on, and the calls continued, and seemed to get no quieter. I turned round, and I realised I was being followed. He was rolling over on his hips, calling as he went. It was an awful sight. And what I can remember now is that I recalled other followers of Jesus who when faced with a lame man in the context of worship had reacted with faith and confidence. The words of the chorus I had sung so often with such enthusiasm at Sunday afternoon Crusader class came back, almost to haunt me: 'Silver and gold have I none, but such as I have give I thee; in the name of Jesus Christ of Nazareth, rise up and walk.' Two thousand years ago that lame man had gone away 'leaping and walking and praising God'.

Now I was the one walking, grateful that our return route through the market-place avoided him, grateful that I could walk quicker than he could roll, and feeling wretched and guilty that my faith and confidence did not quite reach the heights of those first disciples. Hours later, as I tried to go to sleep, the rolling beggar was the image of the day that dominated my thoughts. The only rationalisation I could cling to was that the reason I had seen this man was because Christians had come to Kamalganj, to work for change, aiming to bring about a community with the resources and the technology to care.

I am not sure how convinced I was then, or even am now. I know I was glad not to be a tourist, just looking. I know I took comfort from the thought that my own work might contribute in some small way. I know that I learned that the experience of helplessness is painful.

There was one more experience awaiting me in Bangladesh. Kamalganj was in the Sylhet district. I learned with interest that it was the area from which many of the Bangladeshi immigrants in Birmingham, my home town, originated. Its links with Britain did not end there.

Not far from Kamalganj there was a British-owned tea estate. The HEED team had been given permission to work there, doing some rudimentary development work, teaching some community health and encouraging the people to start simple vegetable gardens. The inhabitants of the estate were not Bengalis; they had been brought from another part of India under the Raj, and now they were effectively trapped on the estate, despised by the Bengalis outside and, even more shocking, living in worse conditions.

Their houses looked worse, run-down, some almost collapsing. The evidence of appearance was confirmed by the doctors, whose tests showed that the incidence of leprosy was higher on the estate than in the surrounding population. It was a well-known fact that leprosy is a disease of poverty. So the reality was that these people, brought here by British commercial interests, were paying the price for our cheap cup of tea.

The HEED staff had discussed the situation with the management of the estate. They explained that they would love to do more, but that would mean charging more for the tea, and then the estate would become uncompetitive. And if the HEED staff didn't like it, they could lump it – right off the estate. So the shareholders got their dividend and the workers got leprosy. A few months later I discovered in James 5 the Bible text with the greatest relevance to the Kamalganj tea estate: *'Now listen, you rich people . . . the cries of those who gather in your crops have reached the ears of the Lord Almighty.'*

3

Ice Cold in Limbo

What else can I do? I cannot go back. I cannot stay here. I am a refugee.

If I could, I would like best of all to have some place for my life.

Laotian refugees, Sob Tuang

Here I was, in a tropical country, wondering if I would ever be warm again. Air-conditioning is wonderful, if you can keep it under control. It is also very confusing. In Bangkok I was still only just coping with the reverse reality of stepping out of a cool and brightly lit building into the hot and sticky night-time. Now I was confused again. The sun was shining, I was in a coach with enormous windows, and I was freezing. It was air-conditioning, but not as I knew it. The nozzles above each seat were fiercely emitting air that felt as if it had been extracted from the deepest deep freeze ever invented.

It did have the advantage of reminding me that I was not dreaming of some half-remembered Sunday-School outing. I had been on some wet ones, I had been on some grey ones . . . but I had never been so cold when the sun was shining. The reason I thought I might be dreaming was that it was 5.00 a.m. Leaping out of a warm comfortable bed at 4.30 a.m. has never been high on my list of luxurious activities, and I had even been offered the opportunity to stay in bed. But reporting that Tearfund had sent me halfway round the world and I had opted for extra sleep rather than see it at work did not seem the best route to universal popularity.

It was the coach full of relentlessly enthusiastic Thai young people that had brought on the Sunday School outing memories. They seemed completely unfazed by the cold. By now I had goose pimples the size of billiard balls on my arms, and I was attempting to stuff tissues into the nozzles to stop the Arctic air flow, while regretting that I had been misled by the sun into wearing only a T-shirt rather than several pullovers. But they were singing choruses. They were stopping for coffee and donuts from Dunkin' Donuts at 5.30 a.m. They were excited, they were happy. I closed my eyes and hoped that the cryogenic technology existed to bring deep-frozen bodies back to life.

The coach sped on from Bangkok, on a remarkably good road. It even began to warm up as the outside temperature climbed. The wholesome enthusiasm of the young people from the YMCA began to remedy the disgust of the night before, when on venturing out of the hotel after dark, I had been accosted by a seedy representative of what appears now to be known as the 'sex-industry'. When I turned down the original offer of a girl, the offers had grown more lurid, more specific and more extreme, at least if watching is considered more extreme than doing. He seemed surprised that I turned him down; I realised that he had taken me for a Western tourist, and I felt a kind of nationalistic nausea at the assumptions he had made on that basis.

After a few hours' journey we arrived. Within seconds the bizarre contradictions of the day became clear. The coach trip was not quite a Sunday School outing. We had headed towards the Cambodian border, a border that in 1980 separated the open peacefulness of Thailand from the Khmer Rouge killing fields. Just a few weeks earlier Cambodians had started to arrive here, not by air-conditioned coach, but on foot, in extremis, close to death.

As I got out of the coach at the gates of Khao-I-Dang refugee camp, with a water tanker turning in, I noted that the countryside looked much the same as it had all the way. There was no geographical indication of the new reality: just serried ranks of refugee huts stretching off into the distance, as far as the eye could see, and a blackboard with a few figures that revealed so much.

The population of the camp was 111,586. That included about 4,500 pregnant women. In the previous twenty-four hours, the blackboard reported, there had been four deaths and eight births. The equivalent of a large town had exploded on to this distant corner of Thailand, and the response had been rapid and to a great extent effective. I asked a young man leaning on the fence by the blackboard if the figures changed much from day to day. 'A few weeks ago,' he replied, 'the death rate was about 250 a day.'

Thailand was my first brush with the relief aid industry. In Bangkok I had seen the downside: relief agencies competing for permission to operate in the refugee camps. Applications had to be in quickly, otherwise someone else would get there first, and they would have the kudos of their name appearing on the TV news at the centre of the action, the front line of the disaster. John Townsend was representing Tearfund at these meetings. He had been a medical missionary in Thailand, and had been almost commuting to Bangkok since the emergency had broken. At the end of the meeting he turned to me and said, 'I think our supporters would rather their money was used making a difference where the need is great, but not where people are falling over themselves to get in first.'

The visit to Khao-I-Dang confirmed his wisdom. Just inside the gates I walked past row upon row of hospital huts, all bearing the name of an international charity. There must have been around ten rows in all, and the blackboard bore witness to their effectiveness in saving lives. No doubt Margaret Thatcher would have seen it as evidence of the benefit of the market economy, competition delivering the goods.

In fact the market economy was evident in other ways. While walking around part of the camp, I came across two men carrying a heavy load slung between two poles. I watched with mounting incredulity as they solemnly unpacked the load and carefully buried it in a hole in the ground, finally covering it over with leaves. It was a block of ice, being delivered to the Coca-Cola stall in the middle of the camp. I was reminded of the comment that the Great Commission to go into all the world was most effectively being carried out by McDonald's and Coca-Cola. How Cambodian refugees paid for their drinks I don't know. But it must have been so uplifting to know that the luxuries of Western culture, best served chilled, were already so close to hand.

Tearfund had taken John's advice. We travelled up north later that week, to visit Sob Tuang, a remote refugee camp in a beautiful hillside setting. These were Laotian refugees. They had been there for years. They were not Cambodians; the TV cameras were not around; no charities were fighting for the right to help them. But their needs were great. A small Tearfund medical team had now begun a healthcare and education programme. It was led by a doctor in his seventies, a former missionary who had come out of retirement to use his gifts once again. Whenever I am asked to challenge young people about mission, I think of this white-haired gentleman who demonstrated so effectively that mission is all about commitment, enthusiasm and obedience, and nothing to do with age.

Within a few days I had received a rapid learning course in refugee camps. In Thailand I had seen the largest camp in the world, small bamboo and sacking huts tightly packed together over a vast piece of open ground; further north, Laotian Hmong tribal people had virtually rebuilt their rural way of life in the beautiful Thai hills, their clothes full of rainbow colours among the lush green of the foliage. Now, in the pulsating urban dynamo of Hong Kong, I met the Vietnamese 'boat people' crowded into almost prison-camp conditions.

Landing by plane in Hong Kong is one of the great adventures of modern air travel, only surpassed by taking off, when the plane appears to be flying between high-rise flats in such a way that you feel you could shout a conversation with the women hanging their washing over the balconies that seem to be no more than a few feet away.

My hosts in Hong Kong were also missionaries who had come out of retirement. John and Esther Fitzstevens were Canadians who had been working in Vietnam with CAMA – the Christian and Missionary Alliance. This was the first, but not the last, time I came across this particular group. I suppose in shorthand it is a US-based denomination, but the thing that impressed me from the start was that it had never made a big division between home and overseas: in British terms it is a denomination and missionary agency all together. Their personnel have been, without fail, a delight to meet; John and Esther set a very high standard.

They were determined that I should have a real taste of Hong Kong. First they took me out for the *dim sum* experience. The great thing was they were very experienced Vietnamese missionaries, but complete novices in Hong Kong. They spoke Vietnamese but not Cantonese. So we were all in the dark together. *Dim sum* is a wonderful Chinese eating tradition, and I am told that eating is a very high cultural activity for the Chinese. I am with them one hundred per cent.

The waiter showed us to a table, and then we realised that trolleys were being pushed round, each packed with small dishes of little morsels. We gathered that if you liked the look of a particular dish, you pointed at it, it was served to you, and you tucked in. Of course the lack of language meant that we had no idea what any dish consisted of. Most of them looked roughly identical: four or five batter-covered balls. The result was that as you bit into them, you had no idea whether the taste was going to be sweet or savoury, delicious or unpalatable. It made the entire meal a culinary adventure, with a kind of built-in frustration factor, because if you found a dish that was absolutely delicious you had very little chance of finding it again. The trolley would come round, and however hard you stared, you had no idea if the taste would be the same as last time.

The highlight came when it was time to pay the bill. The waiter came to the table and collected all our leftover dishes, neatly arranging them according to size. That was when we discovered that size really did matter. Each size plate was charged at a different price, so that adding up the bill was simply a matter of adding up each pile of plates and then adding the totals together. The whole experience had been relaxed and civilised.

There were two other meals in Hong Kong that revealed rather less of Chinese civilisation. John and Esther had discovered a restaurant well off the tourist beat, so that I could have the authentic Hong Kong experience. Authentic in this case meant no English and no knives and forks. Chopsticks are interesting, even entertaining, but for the novice a relatively inefficient way of transferring food from plate to mouth. My efforts drew the cooks from the kitchen to watch. They were convulsed with mirth, pointing at us and bursting into squeals of laughter at my most ineffective efforts.

The entertainment was mutual, the inevitable result of cross-cultural misunderstanding. Our tea was served by the waiter, who stood at one point on the round table and aimed at our cups from a distance. His aim was not always that good, and very quickly the tablecloth was decorated with little damp streams of tea, all of which ended in a teacup. The tablecloth obviously worked rather differently in Chinese culture. I had carefully balanced all my chicken bones around the dish, which seemed very poorly designed for the purpose. I then discovered it had not been designed for that purpose. The waiter arrived to clear the table. He simply tipped all the bones on to the tea-stained cloth, removed the bowls and then removed the cloth, bones and all, with a considerable flourish. We left amid much bowing and smiles, a thoroughly good time having been had by all.

These excursions into Chinese culinary life over, it remained for John and Esther to introduce me to Vietnamese cuisine, or at least as much of it as they could reproduce in their tiny flat. They chose a kind of boiled fondue. A central utensil had a burner in the middle, surrounded by a ring of metal which was filled with water and a variety of spices and vegetables. The idea was that you put a piece of meat or fish in a little wire mesh bowl on the end of a handle, then placed it in the liquid so that it cooked, and added its juices to the soup, which you consumed with the meat as you went along.

There was only one problem. The burner required fuel to burn to keep the liquid boiling. I am not sure if it was supposed to have charcoal, but it clearly was not designed for the only fuel John and Esther had available: cotton wool balls soaked in methylated spirit. The result was spectacular but ineffective. The match would be applied, flames would roar upwards, the water would boil, and after about twenty seconds it was all over, time to start again. It was pretty good as a firework, slightly less so as a cooking device.

Around these various meal tables the Fitzstevens unfolded their own story and the story of the boat people. When they realised that large numbers of Vietnamese people were arriving in Hong Kong by boat, they also realised they had a new opportunity to reach the people whose country they had been forced to leave as the Vietnam war ended. Despite now being past retirement age, they left Canada and came to Hong Kong.

Their experience was an object lesson in itself. They came to Hong Kong to preach the gospel to a people they loved. They discovered, when they went down to the quayside to welcome the refugees coming off the boats after their voyage, that love demanded more than preaching. People were traumatised, they were often sick, they were hungry – and they had nothing. John and Esther got permission from the authorities to greet each new arrival with what they rather endearingly called a 'love bucket'.

The bucket was for collecting water from the communal taps; but they filled it with other essentials: soap, toothpaste and toothbrush, toilet paper – all sorts of things to make the refugees feel that someone cared. They included a simple Vietnamese–English phrase book, and a John's gospel. It was the simplest possible approach to holistic mission, and it genuinely sprang from love rather than theological theory.

The thrill for the Fitzstevens was that this turned out to be the start, not the end. Tearfund had helped to provide a multi-purpose centre for refugees to attend, a place where they could learn English, do some sewing and other activities, and a place where they could worship if they wished. And many of them did. John showed me pages upon pages of transcripts of the stories told by boat people refugees as their testimony before they were baptised. They were being baptised in their hundreds: over fifty at one service the Sunday before we arrived.

The stories were remarkable. They revealed the horror of the voyages many had made. Pirates looked out for the tiny boats, ready to steal any possessions that people had managed to bring with them, and often ready to rape the women on board. Storms were a constant threat. Many of the stories told of boats that capsized, of survivors unable to climb on board other boats already overcrowded, of boats having to sail on leaving the cries of the drowning behind them.

The stories also told of how these people had found God in the middle of their suffering. They came from North Vietnam, many with no awareness of Christianity, or even of God. I remember one who reported that at the peak of the storm he had called out into the wind, crying out to be saved. It was only when he arrived in Hong Kong after his time in quarantine at sea, and was greeted by John Fitzstevens presenting him with his love bucket with the simple sentence, 'This comes from people who love you because God loves you,' that he discovered that the word he had used in his moment of desperation was the same as the word for God, whose name he had never heard before.

Another spoke of how he had set out in search of freedom, and now he had found a freedom he had never known could exist, the freedom that came from faith in Christ. Story after story followed a similar pattern. I knew that sociologists reported analytically that people often change their religious beliefs and allegiance at times of movement and stress. But it was quite a different matter to hear individuals talk of their own reality, their own experience. For John and Esther it was a moving and exciting return to their ministry. John thought that more Vietnamese people had become Christians in a few months in Hong Kong than in all his years in Vietnam. A gospel that was love shown in more than words was bearing fruit.

It was relatively difficult to visit and see the refugees in their camps. Permissions had to be sought, but it was clear that the Fitzstevens' reputation with the authorities was very high, and so I was allowed into a camp that was situated just at the end of the airport runway. Planes roared overhead; it was cold. Women were queuing at taps to collect water, many carrying brightly coloured buckets, presumably love buckets. Many of the men were outside. At this stage of the boat people saga many of the camps were open, with people allowed to come and go and take jobs in the booming Hong Kong economy.

It must have been a curious existence. The workers would come home; home consisted of a three-tier bunk, positioned about one metre from another family home, another three-tier bunk. But home they were. Material curtained off many of the bunks, in a desperate attempt to gain a little privacy and provide a little

28

home furnishing self-expression. Children played on the bottom bunks. Rice cookers boiled away between the bunks. To complete the surreal effect, many had fourteen-inch televisions in one corner, running off car batteries placed under the bottom bunk. Well, if you were earning, what would you spend your money on to make a three-tier bunk seem homely?

I walked through this crowded wonderland and caught the sound of a familiar voice echoing from the corner of a bunk: Larry Hagman at his scheming best as J.R. in *Dallas*. The ranch at Southfork appeared in all its glory, quickly followed by Sue-Ellen dressing for the Oil Barons' Ball. Within minutes I was asking one lady what her hopes were for the future. Esther translated her answer: 'We hope to go to America.' What a surprise. For people in limbo, it was easy for America on television to look like heaven.

4

Flowing with Milk and Honey

Sri Lanka sits like a teardrop at the southerly tip of the Indian sub-continent.

It is a precious jewel of an island, lush and green, with a densely jungled interior and miles of pristine sandy beaches set in a sparkling sapphire sea.

From its ancient name Serendib comes our word 'serendipity', meaning 'happy and unexpected discovery'.

Holiday brochure

Some people think Singapore is heaven: I have to say it troubled me. First, at a serious level, in that it raised deep questions about what development was all about. Here was a country that had virtually eliminated poverty. It was clean, it was almost antiseptic. Hundred-dollar fines for dropping gum on the pavement might seem a touch draconian, but they appeared to work. But then India still had poverty, still had dirt, but also seemed to have more soul. Or was I just a poverty tourist, who found human degradation more colourful and interesting than health and wealth?

Health and wealth were the underlying themes of the second problem. We arrived at Singapore airport en route to Sri Lanka with Frank's suitcases bulging with his ever-growing collection of Tearcraft samples. For the first time the check-in person seemed to notice. Singapore Airlines knew excess baggage when they saw it. This was when I first discovered the potential disaster of excess baggage. They were seriously going to charge us 1 per cent of the first class fare for every kilo over. My face went ashen trying to work out just how much this might be.

Frank was brilliant. Frank was unfazed, and rose magnificently to the occasion. If he had ever kissed the Blarney Stone, this was when he got value for money. We started a lot of kilos over. The first tack was to gently explain what made up the excess baggage. We worked for a relief agency. These supplies were vital; they were going to make all the difference to some very poor people.

So now we were reckoned to be slightly fewer kilos over. Frank kept going. He was patient. He was persuasive. He was holding up the queue. The lady the other side of the counter played her trump card. The whole point of the excess baggage rules, she explained, was passenger safety. The weight of the plane was vital; keeping it down made it safer.

This was my moment to make a telling point. How, I mused, did paying money make it safer? I was very proud of this unanswerable logic. It seemed to fluster her slightly. She now attempted three things at once. She pressed the button which sent our luggage off to the hold. She decided it could be reckoned even fewer kilos over. And she came out with the immortal line, 'You are flying a DC10, you know.' There was a puzzled silence. Then Frank and I realised that she was still trying to defend her safety argument. A DC10 had recently crashed; clearly not enough people had paid up in full for their excess baggage.

Perhaps she realised that she was now on a very sticky wicket. Or perhaps it was just her tea-break. Whatever the reason, she left. She had gone. Our luggage had gone. And so had every record of what it had originally weighed. The new check-in clerk only had a note saying we had to pay for ten kilos of excess baggage. Frank started again with his soft Irish voice in its most persuasive mode. It did not take long. She couldn't understand: if we were only this small amount over, what was all the fuss about?

She handed us our boarding cards, no excess baggage to pay. And, amazingly, that DC10 still made it safely to its destination.

It was my twenty-ninth birthday. It was memorable. So memorable, in fact, that when I am asked to recall my most embarrassing moment I have no difficulty. Sri Lanka, 12 February 1980. I can feel the colour rising to my cheeks even now.

Frank and I had flown on from Singapore to Colombo, the capital of Sri Lanka. One of the country's most endearing features was very quickly revealed to us – the fleet of taxis, all Morris Minors, crowded round the exit from the airport. Now I know there are many who still feel a deep attachment to these particular vehicles; in my experience the attachment has often extended to the slightly disturbing practice of bestowing a name on the one they owned.

I never discovered whether this was a practice taken up by the local taxi-drivers. What I did discover was that they had a severe practical limitation as a taxi, particularly for arriving at an international airport when travelling with Frank and his excess baggage. We literally piled in. Frank and I got in the back, while the driver and his mate discovered, presumably not for the first time, the inadequacies of the Morris Minor boot. We sat there, watching, outwardly cool, as items of luggage flew past the window and on to the roof. After a lot of shouting and a minimum of fixing we set off.

Our steady and stately progress down the road from the airport was suddenly interrupted. A piece of luggage gave up the uneven struggle, said goodbye to the roof, bounced off the rear bumper and deposited itself in the middle of the road. The car lurched to a halt. The mate leapt out and went back to retrieve the case. The driver made straight for the adjacent telegraph pole, which had a length of string tightly wrapped around it. He found the end, untied it, and unrolled a few feet, with which he proceeded to make a rather better job of attaching the case to the roof.

He climbed back into the taxi, and off we went. The whole episode only lasted a few minutes, and it took a moment or two to fully take in its positively surreal dimension. Questions suddenly rose all around. Was there a supply of string on every Sri Lankan telegraph pole? Or was this the place where the luggage on the roof always fell off, and the driver had prepared accordingly? Perhaps, simply, it was a miraculous provision.

Whatever the truth, the string did its job and we were safely delivered to the Holiday Inn hotel. I slept well, but when Frank arrived for breakfast I sensed that his experience had been slightly different. 'I shall never stay in a Holiday Inn again,' he said. He was not a happy man. He had just fallen asleep when his phone had rung. It was Lulu. She wondered if there was anything he needed. Since the answer was uninterrupted sleep, she had already lost the contract. An hour later, Frank had once again just fallen asleep when his phone rang. Another sultry female voice politely enquired whether Lulu had finished yet.

This was definitely an insult being added to injury, but the night was not yet over. At about 5.00 a.m., with sleep having been finally regained, Frank had received an unsolicited wake-up call from reception, who were under the impression he was an Aeroflot pilot. Perhaps Lulu and her friend had been similarly misinformed; whatever the reason, I attempted to offer Frank appropriate sympathy, while slightly jealous that he had been so much in demand. While the postman may always ring twice, that is – in my experience at least – twice more than the hotel room bedside telephone ever manages, even on my birthday.

We set out in one of the ubiquitous Morris Minors to make our visit to Gospel House Handicrafts, the reason for Sri Lanka being in our itinerary. It was about forty-five minutes down the road, a small set of buildings established with Tearfund's help, a fact proudly and unusually acknowledged by a large sign at the entrance. Unusual, because by supporting local Christian partners the intention is for the project to be owned locally, and there are very few 'Tearfund' signs to be found around the world. But John Karunaratne was so pleased with the support he had received that he wanted everyone to know, hence the sign.

His story was remarkable. He had been concerned about the impact of poverty in his home area, poverty that both resulted from and led to a desperate lack of employment opportunities. As he saw young men hanging around, out of work and with nothing to do, he was moved to do something for them. His motivation was the desire both to see them make something of their gifts and lives, and also to prevent them turning to crime as a means of making money.

He had very little resource himself, apart from his passion and his ingenuity. He gave up his own secure job to commit himself to making a difference. The motor from an old disused washing machine became the basis of a wood-turning lathe; that became the basis of a home industry. The home was tiny. His own family vacated bedrooms to make room for machinery and employees. The first group of young men accepted the invitation to learn a trade and make a living.

Before long, their close proximity to a man of such radical and compassionate faith had resulted in their acceptance of a further invitation to trust Jesus Christ for themselves. The ripples began to spread. As Tearfund provided funds to enable the business to disentangle itself from the home into small purpose-built workshops, so John was able to take on more employees, and make a greater impact. The local Buddhist priest was alarmed and joined forces with the local Roman Catholic priest to try and close this evangelical threat to the status quo. The Catholic priest was moved to suggest his flock should read the Bible for themselves in order to counteract this threat – a proposal that absolutely delighted John Karunaratne.

We were welcomed with tremendous enthusiasm. Not for the first time I discovered that representing Tearfund abroad results in being the personal beneficiary of thanks that more properly belong to generous supporters. Occasionally this can be embarrassing, both on a personal level – excuse me, but I haven't really done a lot to deserve this – and also on an organisational, almost philosophical level. The wealthy white charitable benefactor is not a role I aspire to; sometimes there is an almost overwhelming desire to launch into a 'this is about justice and sharing resources, not about charity' explanation. But then I have also had to learn that receiving thanks graciously may be a part of genuine relationship and fellowship; and I have resolved to ensure that I take every opportunity to pass on the thanks to those who really deserve them.

The welcome and hospitality did not end with thanks. It extended to a tour of the buildings, an explanation of the various wood-working processes that were taking place, and a display of prototype products for Frank to examine, comment on and eventually order. Gospel House Handicrafts was specialising in simple wooden toys and jigsaws, and very good they were too. The problem was, of course, that back in Britain they had to compete on price with mass-produced machine-made products, originating from other Asian sources with very low labour costs. Nonetheless, the quality of design and finish was impressive, and the enthusiasm of the work-force infectious.

I felt an enormous privilege. I had met many others who had given their time to selling Tearcraft as voluntary reps. Susan, and some of our closest friends, had spent hours and hours packing and unpacking, pricing, selling; now I was seeing for myself the value of all that labour. The difference it made to needy people. The dignity and hope that meaningful work brought to individuals and community. The opportunity for witness to the creativity and love of God that it represented. On a trestle table in a church hall in Croydon it just looked like another range of products, arranged amateurishly, there to be judged on price and quality. Here in Sri Lanka was the other reality: one family's God-given vision bringing both material and eternal benefit.

Then it was refreshment time. Local and fresh was to be the hallmark. We were taken outside and stood at the foot of some palm trees. One of the young men stripped to a loincloth, stuck a machete through its waistband and began to shin up the tree. As I watched this athletic feat through the movie camera's viewfinder I wondered how close I was to making a X-rated feature. The machete was sharp; the waistband was no more than the strip of cloth stretched tightly round the waist. The strenuous and energetic leg movements required to climb the tree seemed specifically designed to ensure that the cloth was sawn into by the blade. I fully expected there to be a sudden tearing sound, and for the loincloth to flutter to the ground.

But he made it safely to the top, about thirty metres up, and within seconds coconuts were raining down. That was not all. There was a shout from above, a furious hacking at a branch, and down it came. Attached to the branch was a curious-looking appendage, about a foot long and a foot wide, rather as if a large teardrop had been stuck on to dangle under the palm fronds. I had never seen anything like it, but there was not much doubt what it was – because the air was filled with the angry buzzing sound of irate bees, who clearly did not appreciate their lunch-time siesta being disturbed by a sudden home demolition followed by a free-fall non-parachute drop.

In fact there were either not too many in that afternoon, or they were too stunned to notice, but the onlookers were spared retaliation. What we were not spared was the enthusiastic insistence that we should discover the delights of fresh milk and honey. I was still recovering from the realisation that coconuts grew as large smooth-skinned green and not hairy brown things – it's not my fault I grew up in Birmingham, where my only experience of coconuts had been as the prize you did not want to win at the Mop, the annual fair down the road at King's Norton Green.

The machete expertly prepared the coconut, and it was handed to me to drink from. There were only two problems: the act of drinking and the result of drinking. The preparation consisted of opening two small holes, one for the liquid to come out, one for the air to go in. The practised way was to adopt a confident stance which allowed the milk to spurt in a jet, homing in unerringly to one's mouth a few inches away, a little like the method used by stereotypical Spaniards to drink wine. The untried amateur was inevitably left giving more pleasure to others than himself.

Missing the mouth was only part of the problem. A beard can perform a useful absorbent function in certain situations. Cleansing it of coconut milk that has missed the target is another matter. I joined in the laughter, happy to pretend that entertainment by incompetence was part of my calling.

The milk that missed was one problem; the milk that made it into my mouth was the other. The basic problem was that it was warm, in fact hot, carefully prepared by being dangled thirty metres up in the midday sun. I made a mental note that coconut milk should be added to the list of drinks, like Coca-Cola and orange juice, that are only really bearable when chilled. But clearly finishing the offering was important, so I continued with the 50/50 approach, still uncertain whether I preferred it in or out, as it were.

But this was only half the feast. The other half was the glue that held the becs' nest on to the palm branch, otherwise known as honey. The branch was trimmed, the wax part of the nest knocked off, and I was handed a kind of nine-inch honey kebab. Now I quite like honey, but I feel it's best with something – Greek yogurt or bread, for example. Neat, washed down with hot coconut milk, is not how I would choose to enjoy it. The heat, the milk and the honey left me feeling distinctly over-sugared and under par.

* * *

When the subject of my birthday came up, I was feeling slightly better. Well, it didn't exactly come up; I must have raised it. I was still young enough to think it was worth mentioning, and I could still remember my first birthday at work, when I generously invited any who wished to join me for a lunch-time drink, and there was not even one of my hard-working school-teaching colleagues who could spare half an hour. This was probably the point when I realised work was different to enjoyment – and I can still milk a tiny drop of sympathy from my wife over this story even now.

The mistake I made with the Karunaratnes was asking them to guess my age. At twenty-nine it seemed a safe and innocent enough way of making conversation. John looked at me very deliberately, and then said, 'Thirty-seven.' I laughed, which seemed the best way of hiding the pain. 'Miles out,' I replied, and before anything else could be said, Noeline, obviously concerned to make up for her husband's embarrassingly inaccurate suggestion, immediately called out, 'Forty.'

Frank now proved his pedigree as an Irish scholar and gentleman. He leaned over towards me, and said quietly and slowly, 'You have to remember that in the East they regard age with respect. They are simply complimenting you on your maturity.' I thought this remarkably convincing and completely reasonable, and in fact very helpful all round.

The Karunaratnes were now trying to think of a birthday treat suitable for this remarkably mature young man. 'Would you like to go to the beach for a swim?' they asked. This was a hitherto unique offer for someone brought up in Birmingham with a February birthday. The alacrity with which I accepted was far more to do with imagining the impact of the report back home than any great love of swimming in the sea. 'Did you have a good trip?' 'Oh, yes, I had a swim in the Indian Ocean on my birthday, you know.' 'Really . . .'

I then almost as quickly remembered the main drawback of

beach swimming. 'What about getting changed?' I thought of my small towel, my large body, my white skin and a possibly crowded beach. I can't remember exactly how it happened, but once I had established that the beach was only a short distance away, it seemed quite sensible to get changed in their house and then walk down to the beach. Again I thought of my small towel, my large body and my white skin and decided that it would be wise to don my dressing gown for this short trip.

It was a pleasant cotton dressing-gown, a tasteful mix of sub-dued red and blue stripes. With my towel round my neck, a hat perched on my head, flip-flops on my feet, I was ready for my short stroll down to the beach. It was not long before I realised I had missed out on two vital pieces of information. The first was that the short walk was actually along a main market street, with busy, bustling stalls hemming in the road from either side. The second was that I had not extracted any definition of the word 'short'.

Within seconds I recognised that I was now the main sight of interest in the entire street. It wasn't that everyone stopped to gaze; it just felt like it. My face reddened to a shade far less tasteful than any in my dressing-gown stripes. I frantically concentrated on the produce on the stalls in an attempt not to think how absurd I must look: that's why I know one stall was selling imported Swiss roll. And I desperately hoped that the beach would be just round the corner.

Perhaps it was. Time has a habit of feeling a different length to reality. It seemed to take about half an hour to force my way through the market crowds, every step a reminder that I would have to return the same way. Eventually the market ended. We crossed a railway line and walked under the line of palm trees that fringed the beach. I caught a glimpse of the rats running about the trees, and heard a voice explaining that they climbed the trees and occasionally gnawed through the stem of the coconut, so that it came crashing down on the unwary passer-by.

I reflected that this aspect of the Indian Ocean beaches was not often highlighted in the exotic holiday brochures.

The silvery sand of the beaches was; and this beach, once past the market and the rats, fully matched the pictures. It swept off to the horizon in both directions, almost completely deserted, and fringing a sea whose colour seemed to redefine blue with a whole new intensity. I removed my dressing-gown and dashed for the water, hoping that my speed would not allow anyone to take in my white whale-like appearance and confident for once that it would not feel like running into a cold shower. It didn't. It was warm, it was pleasant. I swam and relaxed. I swam and relaxed a little more. I stayed in the water for a long time. This was my February birthday treat. I even managed to forget for a few minutes that I still had to walk back, past the rats and the market. I decided rats were quite fun after all.

5

In the Bleak Midwinter

On the road to freedom
On the road to freedom
Give him back humanity
Let him know his worth
in his father's eyes.

Garth Hewitt

My first overseas visit was over. Six countries in three weeks.
Stories to tell, some to keep quiet about, 8mm film to show. I
travelled round the country, speaking in church halls and home
groups, family services and evensong. I could tell people who
were buying Tearcraft the difference their purchase would make.
I could illustrate exactly how gifts to Tearfund could save lives
and support those sharing the gospel in word and deed. Murphy's
law, of course, meant that in the Brethren Assembly where I had
grown up, with my parents in proud attendance, the projector
broke down.

I think the stories helped. They brought the work of the charity
to life. At the same time I became aware of a curious way in
which some people would use the stories to distance themselves
from the reality. 'It must make such a difference to go and see for
yourself,' they would say. Had seeing for myself made such a
difference? In one sense it had not. I had seen nothing that I did
not know about in theory already. I had been passionate about

Christian concern for the Third World before I went; I had not needed sight to generate conviction. Even emotion and genuine compassion were surely not dependent on personal experience? 'Blessed are those,' said Jesus in only a slightly different context, 'who have not seen and yet have believed.'

What I had begun to gain was the hint that while most people could be made to feel uncomfortable about their wealth by simply talking about the poverty of billions, and that this might generate a response of guilt-assuagement – 'If I put £5 in the Tearfund box can I forget the poor and get on with the rest of my life?' – there was perhaps more to be said for trying to communicate something of the excitement of the opportunity to share in the work of Christians who were making a real difference in their own country. I tried to cut down on the statistics of contrast, and emphasise rather that God was at work through his people, and we could all be a part of it.

Subsequently a survey I organised of attitudes to mission among church leaders and church members revealed that 87 per cent 'often felt overwhelmed in the face of world need'. That is why I have regularly introduced churches to a tiny double-ended plastic spoon. It cost me 10p – and it saves lives. The commonest cause of death in the world today is dehydration in infants as the result of diarrhoea; the two ends of the spoon are measures for salt and sugar, which when added to a cup of water and dispensed every twenty minutes provide life-saving rehydration therapy. Whenever I feel overwhelmed, I remember that 10p can save a life.

That was what lay behind the concept of *The Road to Freedom* – finding a positive high-quality way of communicating a high-quality message. Travel to gather the illustrative stories; come back and through interview, songs and visuals communicate enthusiastically, effectively and positively. Tony Neeves, who as Tearfund's Communications Director and later as head of his own company had already established Tearfund's reputation for quality communication resources at a time when missionary communication was a byword for naffness, came to organise and take the photographs. Garth Hewitt came to gather stories and impressions to turn into his own inimitable style of direct, simple and powerful songs. I came to fill in the gaps, carry the bags and generally be led astray.

Once again the destination was India. Once again I had the delight of leaving a Britain gripped in the cold and damp of winter to head for the heat. The pace was frenetic, the stories dramatic, the impact immense.

We started in the early morning – 6.30 a.m. to pick up Garth. We shared the flight with John Denver – two guitar-playing songwriters on one plane, but he was flying first class, and Garth Hewitt was not. We arrived in Delhi once again in the middle of the night, and finally made it to our hotel at 2.00 a.m. I am not sure it was worth it. I had not actually fallen asleep when the alarm went off at 5.30 a.m., and we were off to the airport again.

Inevitably, since we had made exceptional efforts to be there in time, the plane was delayed. We sat in the departure lounge, having met up with our Indian travelling companion, H.P. George. He was a wonderful character. He assured me that his initials stood for Horse Power, and with his thin grey moustache bristling at every scent of anything that needed organising or sorting, he was certainly full of energy. That morning he also displayed enormous faith.

We had heard that there had been a cyclone disaster in the state of Gujerat. H.P. assured us that the Discipleship Centre, for whom he worked as co-ordinator for relief and development, were involved in emergency relief. We thought it was worth investigating whether a visit to Gujerat could be squeezed into our already busy schedule. H.P.'s faith was demonstrated when he pulled out an Indian Airlines timetable. There was something deeply ironic about consulting an air timetable while waiting for a delayed flight – especially when we discovered that two recent Indian Airlines crashes had affected their entire schedules. But H.P. concluded that it could be done by cutting short the first stage of the itinerary, and by making use of a train so we could catch a plane. He made it all sound so straightforward.

Eventually the plane was ready, and we flew to Kanpur as planned. We had an afternoon to stroll around the town, and two things caught my attention. One was the cows, the sacred cows. There were not hundreds of them, but their lazy wanderings in the busy streets of a major town still seemed bizarre, symbolic of what to some is the slightly endearing chaos of India, to others its infuriating mix of ancient and modern.

The other thing that caught my attention perhaps similarly reflected that same mix: a giant advertising hoarding dominated by the face of a serious young man, his suit and contrasting modern tie suggesting someone up to date and yet worthy of trust. Under the picture there was a mass of (to me) incomprehensible Indian script, in which two English words in block capitals stood out (to me) remarkably clearly: 'SEX SPECIALIST'. I was disappointed not to be able to understand the rest of the poster, and could only reflect on the apparent purity of a language that did not have a word for this particular profession – or perhaps the English gave the impression of additional authority in this field of work. Interestingly this poster was juxtaposed with another, all in English, for Dunlop radial tyres, which carried the slogan 'Miles ahead in performance'.

This afternoon stroll was the leisurely lull before the hectic storm. The next morning at 7.00 a.m. our mini-fleet of black Hindustani Ambassador taxis – living industrial archaelogy of the Morris Oxford variety – set off for the town of Hamirpur. It was my first experience of rural India, and it made a deep impression. The taxis parked just on the edge of a village called Sikrodi outside the town, and we walked down the path past the mud-brick houses. On every side there were little cameos, every glimpse a timeless tableau. Donkeys tethered to a post; bullock carts with hand-carved wheels, some piled with firewood; women shimmering past, covered from head to toe in saris the colours of the rainbow, with brass water pots balanced apparently effortlessly on their heads; old men sitting on rickety wooden bed-frames outside their homes; women stirring the cooking pots over slowly burning wood fires.

As we turned another corner someone mentioned that the village had been on this site for six thousand years. At the same time I caught a glimpse of a young woman, surely no more than fifteen, tenderly gazing down at the tiny baby that suckled at her breast, while a few feet away a cow gazed contentedly over the low wall of its pen. Suddenly it struck me: we were walking into Bethlehem.

We had left London just geared up for the commercial Christmas shopping spree. The lights were being switched on, the trees going up, the images of snow, reindeer and Father Christmas beginning their seasonal take-over. And two days later, here were the real images, timeless reflections of ancient truth. At that moment I gained a simple insight, but one which I have become convinced has profound implications for Christians in the West: the Bible was written in a Third World situation.

The confirmation was just around the next corner. The path between the houses opened up to a large open space at the centre of which was the well. It was on a slightly raised platform, and surrounded by children with buckets, men washing clothes, women talking animatedly and bullocks with carts. The Samaritan woman would have recognised the scene. When we read John 4, we have to resort to commentaries, the preacher to long explanations, so that we understand the cultural significance of the story. The women at the well in an Indian village have some definite advantages, in this area at least. It was a scene so full of life and colour that we made it a fold-out poster on one side of *The Road to Freedom* tour programme.

* * *

The reason we had come to Hamirpur was that it had experienced one of the more obvious disadvantages of being a Third World location. A few weeks earlier it had been devastated when the River Jamuna burst its banks; 81,000 people had lost their houses and property in the area. The Discipleship Centre had been asked to be part of the official relief effort and care for 2,000 families, and that afternoon Garth and I, slightly self-consciously, helped to hand out some of the blankets and clothing paid for by Tearfund supporters. We overheard an official's comment: 'This is the largest gift some of these people have ever received in their lives.' In one sense it seemed so little. We were introduced to Gangaram, a dignified old man who received his bundle and then showed us his home, still showing signs of the damage the floods had caused. His possessions had been washed away.

H.P. George encouraged us with another slant on the story. Four years earlier floods had caused similar damage in another part of India. Tearfund had given a grant for the reconstruction of houses, but the Discipleship Centre, having become involved, realised that the people of Burari needed more than just reconstruction of their homes. They were dependent on low-paid seasonal work in the fields, and struggled for survival for long periods of the year.

The Discipleship Centre asked Tearfund to provide ten sewing machines as a start-up grant; the government then backed this with many more, and Burari began a thriving tailoring industry. When the Discipleship Centre wanted clothing for their emergency relief at Hamirpur, they went back to Burari. The garments I handed out that afternoon had been made by the victims of previous flooding; the help they had received had enabled them to help others.

Now began the attempt to make the extra visit. The reason was simple; we had visited an area of flood relief, but a few weeks later the damaged corner of Gangaram's house was about the only sign of the disaster. Perhaps the more immediate cyclone in Gujerat would offer a better illustration of the devastation flooding brings.

So the three taxis set off back towards Kanpur. After a total of three breakdowns, two of them made it back in time for us to catch the train. After Indian Airlines and Indian taxis we were ready to give Indian Railways their chance. It was an overnight train, so we had a sleeping compartment booked for us. It was clean and comfortable, and Garth sat up on the top bunk strumming his guitar encouraging a new song to emerge. This drew the conductor along to our door to ask him to stop, as there were passengers trying to get to sleep. A moment to treasure.

The train arrived at Delhi at 5.00 a.m. The station was heaving with people. What it was like in the rush hour I preferred not to contemplate. At least H.P. was firing on all cylinders. He organised us and our luggage, which we suddenly noticed had appeared on the head of a tall porter. Garth's guitar case seemed to be about fifteen feet off the ground, perched atop various suitcases. It was a kind of lighthouse beacon, steering us bleary-eyed through the crowds.

We piled into another taxi and arrived at a house belonging to Barry Mackey, the India director for World Relief, the US equivalent of Tearfund. Despite the hour a delightful breakfast was served, but within minutes we were on our way to the airport, and caught an early flight to Bombay. Here there was another delay while we once again waited for the connecting flight. This was when Garth woke up. He remembered the train and being asked to stop singing. But he was now in an airport. The train had been going to Delhi and he was now in Bombay. Delhi station, breakfast with Barry? No recollection at all. I made a mental note of the potential strength of sleeping tablets and realised why he had made no protest about the flight of his guitar through Delhi station.

We arrived at Bhavnagar at 3.00 p.m. and then had a two-and-a-half-hour drive to the site of the cyclone. We came to the village of Vankiya just as it was getting dark, but not before we could see signs of the damage. Trees had been uprooted, and most disconcerting, the foundation of the railway tracks had been washed away, leaving bent and distorted rails rather drunkenly wiggling off into the distance.

So far as I knew we were completely unexpected visitors, but the Patel family, who were clearly significant in the village, were more than willing to entertain us. They served us a delightful meal, washed down with a glass of water, which since it was neither bottled nor boiled was itself accompanied by a prayer. There was no electricity; we ate in the courtyard of the home, lit by the glow of the fire and the hurricane lamps. It was a miracle of peace and contentment at the end of a day of travel. Garth sang some songs to round off the day. He too must have caught the Christmas spirit from Hamirpur, and even 'In the Bleak Midwinter' seemed to make sense at the time.

The peaceful hospitality was in stark contrast to the story they told. Just three weeks earlier their state authorities had been appealing for help with drought relief. Then rain had come. It rained continuously for two days, then during the afternoon the wind blew stronger and stronger. As it got dark the electricity failed, and the whole village was plunged into darkness. The rain lashed down as the wind reached speeds of 120 m.p.h. People in the village were screaming with fear.

At 8.00 p.m. the water level at the nearby Khodiar dam was rising alarmingly. When the power failed throughout the region the authorities at the dam panicked and opened the sluice gates. Within seconds an eight foot wall of water had crashed down on Vankiya. Large parts of the village were simply washed away. Scores of people had drowned.

Early the next morning we returned to the village to take pictures so we could illustrate the tragedy. I was taken to meet

Gobar Madha. The rest of the villagers thought we would want to hear his story. He was sitting on a wall, unmoving, his eyes empty and staring. A little boy sat on his knee. Gabaru was five years old. When Gobar Madha heard the roar of the approaching water somehow he had grabbed Gabaru and started to climb a tree. The water had surged round him, and he had felt the current tugging at his son's body.

In his desperation he was using both his hands to cling to the tree. He had sunk his teeth into the boy's shoulder, and for two hours they had held on together until the wind and the water began to drop. When it was safe to come down from the tree, Gobar Madha had discovered that his wife, brother, sister-in-law and eleven children had all been swept away and drowned. All that remained of his extended family was himself and Gabaru. Gobar Madha still sat, seemingly almost in shock. One of the villagers opened Gabaru's shirt so we could see the scars in his shoulder, a kind of fatherly stigmata, the marks of salvation.

The village still bore the scars as well. Houses completely demolished, uprooted trees trapped against walls. As I walked down the street I was greeted by a young man in army uniform. He insisted that I join him for a cup of tea. It seemed churlish to refuse, even though I normally don't drink tea. I need not have worried. This was not Tunbridge Wells tea-room tea. This was the real Indian version. Condensed milk, sugar, water, a few herbs, all boiled up together. It was a heady brew, and to me almost completely undrinkable.

I listened to the soldier's broken English, explaining that he had come home when he had heard about the cyclone because that was the only way to discover whether his family had survived. I confess I was also anxiously wondering, desperately hoping, that one of the team would come round the corner and tell me it was time to go. They did, but not in time to save me. I have retained a pathological fear of tin mugs to this day.

To get back on schedule we had a plane to catch. We left

Vankiya at the last possible moment, saying goodbye to H.P. George, who was staying to see what further help could be given. The drive back to Bhavnagar was fast and tense. Would we make it in time? But this was Indian Airlines. We just made it for the scheduled departure time, but there was no sign of a plane. There were, however, plenty of passengers, and we discovered we were not guaranteed a seat. So now the waiting became tense. We went to the desk to check the situation. We sat down and tried not to glare at further arrivals. The realisation that if either the plane did not come, or we did not get on it, the whole itinerary would be blown, made us very nervous. We even began to debate who should be left behind if only some seats became available. It was not much of a debate. Tony and Garth were agreed that sacrifice was the junior staff member's responsibility. But eventually the plane came . . . and we got the last seats.

6

Moved with Compassion

> *To feel your compassion*
> *To weep with your tears*
> *Come soften my heart, O Lord, soften my heart.*
> Graham Kendrick

We arrived in Calcutta, to be met by Vijayan Pavamani whom I knew well from my first few weeks at Tearfund, when he and his wife Premila had been special guests for our tenth anniversary tour and I had driven them round much of England. They were, and are, a remarkable couple, deeply committed to the gospel and seeing it demonstrated in sacrificial love for those in need. They had begun a home for alcoholics and drug addicts in Calcutta, they were leaders of a church and later they also began a home for the children who had been abandoned and lived on the platforms of Howrah station.

Vijayan had got to know Mother Teresa well. There was mutual respect for the work they were doing, and occasionally one would refer people in need to the other so they could receive the most appropriate care. Thus he had felt able to ask if she would meet us during our brief stay, and so we began our visit to Calcutta by calling at one of the most famously undistinguished front doors in the world. One of the sisters showed us in, and after a short pause we were taken up to the balcony to meet her.

The immediate impression was just how tiny and frail she

appeared, an impression quickly supplemented by the realisation of the animation and humour of her conversation. When she discovered we were from England she expressed her delight at the news that Malcolm Muggeridge – 'dear Malcolm' – had finally joined the Roman Catholic Church, news that had broken only that morning. She graciously accepted our gift of a Tearfund calendar for the coming year, which featured photographs that Tony had taken on previous overseas visits. 'I like this,' she said, 'your pictures give dignity back to the poor.' Garth gave her one of his cassettes, and with a twinkle in her eye she explained that she was terribly sorry that she could not ask him to sing, but the sisters had taken a vow of silence for the day.

There seemed to be a potential logical gap in this reasoning, but my ego had not yet reached the point where I felt I could or should challenge Mother Teresa's powers of rational thinking. Rather I found myself playing the part of 'man impressed by being in presence of celebrity': Tony took my picture with her (who knows, one day it might be useful to include in a book and make me look important) and I asked her to sign Susan's Bible – a pocket one I used on overseas visits. 'Be holy, for Jesus who loves you is holy,' she wrote.

After forty minutes the audience was over. She had been completely unassuming and completely at ease, even though she must have known that we were doing little more than regarding her as one of the sights of Calcutta. And of course I plead guilty to the charge of name-dropping. It's amazing how much mileage one can make out of forty minutes. I am not sure I can claim any justification from the fact that others, some world-famous in their own right, have done the same. I have even made a half-hearted attempt to collect other signatures in my Bible, Christians who have impressed me but whose names will not impress others.

The saving grace is this: Mother Teresa became the most famous Christian in the world, and she became famous for caring for the poor. Her celebrity status was founded on genuine worth, her fame earned by a lifetime of service. Vijayan Pavamani said to me later that day 'Because of Mother Teresa everyone in India associates Christianity with care for the poor.' What an epitaph. One billion people left with a Christ-like impression of Christ. The photo Tony took that day is a treasured possession; there is a radiant inner beauty that transcends the wrinkles of age.

So when I have dropped her name, I hope that occasionally I have at least encouraged others to reflect on the basis of her fame, and what it really means to be a follower of Jesus. As Tony Campolo memorably put it in a Tearfund video I produced: 'They gave Mother Teresa a Nobel prize for doing what every Christian is supposed to do.'

We left the Mother House and drove out to the Arunoday Midway Home. Arunoday means sunrise; the home was the place where Vijayan and Premila worked to give a new hope of dawn to those gripped by addiction. As we drove through Calcutta it was hard to grasp the extent of addiction within a city gripped by poverty. Some of their clients were middle-class Indians who had succumbed to alcohol or harder drugs much as some middle-class people do the world over. Others were those who had taken the chemical route to escape from poverty, and discovered it was a dead end.

Vijayan and Premila were the only source of rehabilitation for such people, certainly in Calcutta, and for much of India. Their methods and commitment had drawn visitors from the highest level of government. They were convinced that Christianity had a powerful role to play in the rehabilitation process. They made Bible study part of the routine in the home, delighting to call it 'spiritual therapy', a description that met with full approval from authorities in a country steeped in religion. It was no magic wand, but there were those in the home who had discovered that an encounter with the living Christ was able to break the hold of addiction and set them on to a positive new basis for life.

The home was on the edge of the city. The drive took us out of the teeming centre of Calcutta, crowded with people, cows, pedal rickshaws and hand-pulled rickshaws, through slightly calmer suburbs, but all suffused with the signs of peeling faded grandeur in the buildings of the Raj. The centre was choking with dust from the building of the underground railway and from the pollution of hundreds of thousands of charcoal fires.

Eventually the buildings became slightly more spaced, the air a little cleaner, and trees began to appear. The home itself, obtained with Tearfund's help, was an oasis of peace. The well-ordered garden (another part of the therapy) had all sorts of fruit trees, and the fishpond was surrounded by trees that offered welcome shade from the heat. We spoke to some of the clients, and heard their stories. It was a privilege that having heard Vijayan describe the home and their work, I now had the opportunity to see for myself.

That drive was about all I was to see of Calcutta, once described by a friend, memorably, as 'literally hell on earth'. When we left the Midway Home the weekend took on a strange shape. Vijayan's itinerary included a meeting with church leaders from Calcutta late that afternoon, to be followed by a special event in the Assemblies of God church in the centre of town. Then the next day, Sunday, there were church services to contribute to before we left for Madras in the afternoon. Knowing that time was short, Garth and Tony were unanimous – I was staff, and staff should do as many of the meetings as possible, allowing them to focus on the real purpose of our visit, the gathering of impressions and pictures.

It was not to be the last time that overseas visits would reveal different agendas for the visitor and the visited. At least with three of us there was a chance to split up and try and meet everyone's agenda requirements. Vijayan was anxious that our visit should help to validate his work and ministry in Calcutta. Christianity in India, particularly evangelical Christianity, has in the past often been middle class, and in reflection of its middle-class and English influence has been suspicious of the so-called 'social gospel'. The fact that Vijayan was also running his own church and was supported by a UK charity that was not really known by others left him vulnerable to isolation and suspicion.

So our visit was a real opportunity for Tearfund's and his own credentials to be introduced and established. Hence the visit to Mother Teresa, hence the other meetings planned. So I set off to meet the church leaders, determined to do my best by Vijayan and Premila; Garth and Tony were taken on a guided tour of the sights and sounds, the streets and stalls, the gutters, the smells, the people, the poverty, the energy and suffering that is Calcutta.

Garth summed up their experience in a memorable song, the title song that opened *The Road to Freedom* presentation. As we toured the country, every night for twenty-four nights I stood in the wings, waiting for my entrance to make the introductions, listening to these evocative words:

> The sights that fly before your eyes
> Can simply drag you down
> I lived a year in Calcutta
> The night I first hit town.
> The sights you see
> They freeze your brain . . .

But I hadn't seen the sights. They hadn't flown before my eyes, my brain was not frozen. So that Saturday evening in Calcutta, Garth arrived at the church to do a concert with his emotions reeling from the sensory impact of the streets, and I arrived extremely nervous about preaching in this curious setting. Curious in that the church was like any other city centre church anywhere in the UK, but the city centre outside was just a little different.

The poster advertising this evening event was truly remarkable. Garth was described as 'Priest turned gospel singer', Tony as 'the media man' – and I too, illustrated by a cut-out photo that left my silhouette looking not unlike a map of India, had turned: 'teacher turned preacher, with the unchanging message'. Garth thought the news had got out that I had only one sermon. I nearly did not have a sermon at all.

That was because there were two points in the evening when that city centre outside broke into the familiar interior. One was when the mosque next door began its heavily amplified call to prayer, the wailing voice apparently relishing the unusual competition of a Garth Hewitt concert. The second came when I was preaching. The door at the back of the church was opened to allow some ventilation into the hot and stuffy church. The result was that I was given my own personal window on the world neatly framed by the open doorway. Men, women, children, cows, rickshaws – all moved past in a kaleidoscope of images. It made concentration difficult.

The next morning 'staff' was still busy. My first appointment was at Carey Baptist Church at 10.00 a.m. I don't think the simple platform and pulpit quite dated back to Carey himself, but there was nonetheless an enormous sense of history. William Carey, the Northampton cobbler, was not only the founder of what became the Baptist Missionary Society, but is also usually regarded as the father of the modern missionary movement as a whole. He arrived in Calcutta in 1793 and worked in India until his death in 1834.

As I preached in the church he had founded, that was about all I knew. I could recall my astonishment that at a mission exhibition where I had represented Tearfund, the Baptist Missionary Society stand had included a glass case with a strand of Carey's hair. Someone once commented to me, inaccurately and unhelpfully, that while Tearfund was about meeting the needs of the poor, BMS followed the example of Carey and focused on preaching the gospel. When we look at history with the false theological spectacles that insist on seeing evangelism and social action as two distinct activities, it is amazing just how distorted our view can become.

William Carey demonstrated that mission is primarily about sharing the love of God. The range of his concerns was broad, his impact astonishing. He translated and/or published the Bible in forty Indian languages and translated Indian religious classics into English; he started schools, he founded the Agricultural Society of India to encourage improvements in farming. He published the first books on science and natural history in India, he established the first newspaper ever printed in any Eastern language. He introduced the Savings Bank to fight the evil of usury. He took a lead in the campaign to abolish widow-burning. 'He is,' say Ruth and Vishal Mangalwadi, his Indian biographers, 'the central character in the story of the modernisation in India.'

I was not allowed to enjoy the privilege of Carey's pulpit for long. As soon as my sermon was finished I was whisked away to Vijayan and Premila's church, Emmanuel, to preach there as well. Curiously, in one weekend in Calcutta, I did about half the total preaching I have done overseas in my entire life. I have never sought such opportunities and I am very reluctant to accept offers. I feel that I have relatively little in terms of experience of the life of faith to offer those who have since birth lived in poverty, struggling for survival. And if I am unsure that I have spoken clearly into another culture when I am in Northern Ireland, then those uncertainties are multiplied in cultures that are not even based on the English language. I am fascinated by those ministers who feel their presence in a place is only validated when they have preached there. I just know that I have learned far more by listening than talking when I travel, far more than I could ever have given.

By late afternoon we were on another plane, this time heading for Madras. We had been in Calcutta less than forty-eight hours, but they had taken their toll emotionally and physically. Garth was not feeling too well, and I was not very far behind. But clearly it was important for staff to keep going and not let our hosts down, so I found myself graciously allowing the others to recover in the hotel while I ventured forth alone to see Tearfund's partners at work in Madras.

The focus was on work in the slums. In Indian cities slums are not the sprawling outer ring of makeshift housing that they are in Africa and Latin America. Here they tend to be smaller and more defined, squeezed on to plots of land left as being of no commercial value, usually because they are marshland, or susceptible to flooding. Often they are surrounded by blocks of flats, or tenement buildings, whose brick solidity mocks the tiny hovels put together with wood and card and sacking, packed tightly together to make the most of the space.

But I could not resist a smile at my first port of call. A sign at the door boldly announced THE JENNIFER EVANS HANDI-CRAFT PROJECT. I had heard that in India they loved to name buildings in honour of their benefactors; members of staff at Tearfund had recounted being asked to open buildings that had been paid for by Tearfund, then discovering their name had been attached to them as if they personally were responsible. Jennifer Evans was, and still is, a delightfully self-effacing colleague, and I knew that she would be extremely embarrassed that her name was up in lights in this way. I was already looking forward to teasing her about it. When I did, she explained that it could have been worse. There were other colleagues, she informed me, who had given their names to toilet blocks.

Inside the project there were twenty-two people making bags and cane furniture. It was almost as dark and depressing as the slum outside, and yet there was a positive atmosphere of hope. You could almost smell it. Simple employment meant some degree of regular income. Regular income gave hope that children would eat, could go to school . . . might even have the opportunity to escape the slum.

That sense of hope did not last long. By the end of the day I had caught up with Garth's Calcutta experience and come face to face with the reality of poverty for myself. It was only a small slum. As before, it was squeezed on to a piece of wasteland between relatively grand apartment buildings. It didn't seem much bigger than a football pitch, yet it had been home to around three hundred families, crowded close together in their rough, makeshift dwellings. It was a disaster waiting to happen. Apparently one family had been using a paraffin stove. It had tipped over, and set their home on fire. In minutes it had spread to the whole slum, moving through the tightly packed houses with great ease and frightening rapidity. In minutes it was all over; the poor do not have much to burn.

That was what I heard. All I saw was a blackened piece of waste ground. In the middle, a solitary figure crouched and huddled, clutching a stick with which he raked desultorily, almost absent-mindedly, through the ashes. He and his family had lived here for years. Every day he went out to collect empty and discarded jute sacks. Any he found he washed, then resold. Most days he made enough from this basic recycling to keep his family going. He began to build up his stock. With no store-room, no room for expansion, he kept his stock on the floor of his home. The whole family lived on their reserves, their savings. All their worldly wealth formed their foundation and their carpet.

The fire had taken it all. Years of work lost in minutes. He crouched in the ashes, enveloped in an invisible haze of grief and despair. I stood in silence, then felt anger welling up inside me. The rage from my student days re-awoke. I wanted to kick, to lash out, to hurt. But who? There was no focus, but there was anger. I was confused and slightly ashamed. It seemed an odd and for me a very unusual emotional reaction.

Years later John Stott, Tearfund's President, came to speak at our weekly staff prayers. He chose the topic of 'motivation' and talked about how Jesus was motivated into action by his reaction to suffering, the result of sin. He talked about his compassion – but he also talked about the Greek word used in the New Testament to describe another dimension of his reaction: he 'snorted with indignation'. So when Jesus was faced with the despair and injustice of human suffering he reacted with anger. I remembered my own reaction that day in Madras, and I felt a tinge of comfort and hope.

7

Living Water

*The World Health Organisation has estimated
that 80% of all sickness and disease in the world
is attributable to impure water or inadequate sanitation.*
                                    Tearfund profile booklet

The next morning it was another fleet of Hindustani Ambassadors, next stop Vellore. It was over three hours' drive through the south India countryside, and the most notable moment came when we crossed an enormous bridge, which appeared to be a bridge over nothing. We got out to look, and saw the evidence of five years of drought. The bridge spanned an enormous river bed, hundreds of feet wide. In the centre there was a tiny trickle, a minute stream. The contrast between expectation and reality could not have been starker.

Expectation and reality clashed on a completely more farcical note when we arrived in Vellore. Vellore is the home of a mission hospital and Christian medical college significant throughout India, training nurses, doctors and medical practitioners of all kinds to a very high standard. They were expecting us.

There was a hand-written flyer attached to a noticeboard. It is best reproduced in its entirety:

> **rand sings**
> today – tuesday, the 7th december '82
> rand – a singer from Cliff Richard's team,
> will be singing and participating
> in the evening devotions
> in the hospital chapel from 6:30 – 7:00 p.m.
> all are invited to join in

Garth found this particularly hysterical. He suggested that the main heading was a misprint, that my name in India was really Rand Singh. Then he indicated his view that as staff my duties clearly extended to meeting all the expectations of our hosts, and therefore I should sing; but to show his goodwill, he would turn up to support me while I attempted to fill this particular engagement. I found his kindness overwhelming.

I felt, however, that my experience of public singing was perhaps too limited for me to face this challenge with equanimity – more accurately, to allow hard-working, God-fearing medical personnel to risk their equanimity. So I explained that if Garth insisted on this course of action, I would be obliged to explain that there had been a terrible misunderstanding, and that while I was more than willing to sing, my name was really Garth Hewitt. The trump card! He quickly agreed to take on the role of my substitute.

I cannot resist explaining, however, that my singing career began as a treble in the school choir in Benjamin Britten's *War Requiem*, and ended at my first Tearfund Christmas party, where I gave a virtuoso performance of my old school song. This begins memorably with a reference to Birmingham: 'Where the iron heart of England throbs beneath its sombre robes' and continues with similar sentiments ('die of service, not of rust') which the Victorians presumably found easier to sing seriously than teenagers of the sixties. I certainly got more laughs that evening than did the artiste who followed, singing his chart-topping hits such as 'Living Doll' and 'Bachelor Boy'. It is nice to be able to claim that I have sung on the same bill as Cliff Richard – whoops, there goes that old name-dropping temptation again.

Our hosts were now EFICOR – the Evangelical Fellowship of India Commission on Relief – in one sense the Indian equivalent of Tearfund, in recent years under C.B. Samuel a tremendous and energetic resource for Christian development. We were due to visit a project that had become very significant to Tearfund: the water drilling-rigs. EFICOR had two, one provided by Tearfund. Supporters responded with enormous enthusiasm to the possibility of raising enough money to sink one well in an Indian village. There was a clearly understood benefit, a neatly finite project and an attainable fund-raising challenge – each well cost around £600 to £1,000.

The drilling-rigs were working not far from Vellore, so we were looking forward to seeing one in action. But we made a poor start. That afternoon we drove to a village. Yes, the rig was there. Yes, the rig was working, drilling away noisily. The problem was there were no people. No one was around, no one seemed very excited about the possibility of fresh water. It was all a bit of an anti-climax.

The next morning we decided to try and find a village where a well had been drilled and a pump installed. Perhaps then we could get the stories and pictures to match the significance of the project. So another drive, and we arrived at another village. Again it seemed slightly deserted, and, just as difficult, the village had been recently 'developed' and consisted of two rows of neat concrete box houses. It was not very typical and not very photogenic.

Our photographer had other things to worry about. No sooner had we arrived than he clutched his stomach and indicated the need to withdraw rapidly. Slightly to our amazement, Garth and I watched Tony being bundled into the Land Rover and driven off at high speed, in a cloud of dust, back down the road we had just come up. Minutes passed. We wondered if we had been abandoned, or if Tony had been kidnapped. More minutes passed. After about half an hour, we saw the cloud of dust reappear on the horizon, and shortly after, Tony was back with us.

Apparently the driver had known there was someone in the next village who was the proud owner of a European-style toilet. Whether he had realised that this acquisition would make him liable to providing the location for a Monty Python sketch was doubtful. There he was, passing the time of day, when a Land Rover came screeching to his door and an Englishman with a look of agony on his face was hurriedly ushered into the presence of his prize possession, only to come rushing out minutes later, jump back into the Land Rover with a yell of 'Thanks' and disappear in a cloud of dust and a clash of gears. One felt that a number of social conventions had not been fully observed.

Things could only get better – and they did. We went in search of the other rig, which was hard at work in the village of Melputhupakam. There were some people here at least, and they seemed pleased with the rig's activity. It was roaring away, a double-act of two brightly painted red and yellow lorries. One was the generator, which provided the power. The other carried the drill itself on its back; on arrival this was hinged back so that the business end could come into contact with the ground.

The front of each lorry bore the simple words: JESUS SAID I AM THE LIVING WATER. But this was not the end of the spiritual content of the well-drilling process. On arrival the crew of six began the process with prayer. This was not a kind of well-meaning nod in God's direction. This was serious, because their prayers were part of the decision-making process that determined exactly where the rig would drill. There was no expensive, highly skilled geological survey. There was a prayer meeting . . . and then they would gather round a map of the village, dangle the bunch of lorry keys above it, and when they stopped spinning round, that was where they would drill.

I suspected that this methodology might provoke theological discussion in some areas of UK evangelicalism, but then so might the apostles drawing lots for the successor to Judas. The fact was, they informed us, in the previous year they had drilled 144 times, and all but twice had struck water. As far as they were concerned, God answers prayer.

As we were watching, we suddenly noticed that there was a hint of dampness around the point where the drill was disappearing into the ground. Tony grabbed his camera, and I started filming on my little Super 8 cine camera. The damp patch quickly turned into a bubbling flow of water, and then, in seconds, it became a high pressure fountain, water spraying into the air. We were immediately drenched, and it was a debatable point whether the Anglicans present had just been fully immersed, or the Baptists simply sprinkled. It was certainly an exhilarating moment. I had seen it on films, when the oil-rig struck oil, and the resulting 'gusher' meant untold wealth. Here it was water, gushing up from fifty metres below the ground, offering the hope of better health for the community.

I spent some time with one family in the community, trying to discover how a new well might affect their life. Munjula was a pretty twelve-year-old with a captivating smile, her hair in bunches decorated with bright purple flowers, and already playing a vital role in the life of her family. She was the first to get up in the morning, at around 5.00 a.m., and one of her first tasks was to collect the water. This meant a long walk through the village, and possibly a long wait, because as low caste she was obliged to give way to anyone high caste who might be present. Then, the full and therefore heavy pot balanced on her head, she would return.

Watching girls and women sway gracefully past with their pots, the immediate reaction was to admire their poise and skill. When I then tried simply to lift the pot, admiration turned to amazement that someone as young and slight as Munjula had the strength and energy to lift it up and on to her head, let alone carry it for any distance, over a mile in this case. It was only later that I read that this practice results in significant back pain and degeneration, a major health problem for Third World women.

Munjula had another weight to carry several times a day: her three year old brother Bathaladu. He was her special responsibility, and she was often left to look after him while her mother and father were out at work. Her father, Appasamy, set out every morning in search of thorn bushes to cut for firewood, which he would bring back to sell in the village. Her mother Mariamma could occasionally get work picking grain in the village fields, in return for which she was allowed to keep some of the crop for herself and her family. On these days Munjula stayed with Bathaladu, only going to school when her mother returned to make it possible for her to set off for her free school dinner.

This was a relatively recent government provision, designed to encourage school attendance, and clearly failing in its immediate intention as far as Munjula was concerned. After lunch it was time to return to the well, this time carrying Bathaladu. There would probably be another trip before her 7.00 p.m. bedtime, so I was not surprised that she seemed pleased that the newly drilled well, finished off with a pump, was in the low-caste end of the village, close to her home. It also promised a regular supply of fresh, clear, pure water, whereas after five years of drought the old village well was beginning to dry up.

We left Melputhupakam after Munjula's school dinner, and set off for another village, Vilapakkam. Even as we arrived we sensed a different atmosphere. People were always curious when English visitors arrived, but here some of the looks seemed more hostile than curious. There was a heaviness about the place that made me feel uneasy.

We were introduced to Lily Chandrasekar. She was sitting on the low wall in front of the veranda of her simple dried-mud home. Next to her was a large framed black and white photograph of a man, black-haired and with a neat moustache. It was a photograph of her husband. Now he was dead. At one point she propped the photo up on a chair, as if she wanted him to sit there once again. Lily told us the story. I asked an initial question; it was interpreted, and it was as if a tap of grief had been turned on. The story poured out. Lily did not wait for individual sentences to be translated. A torrent of words emerged with an intense passion, her eyes staring into the middle distance, focused on the past and not the present.

He had been the village school teacher, an active Christian – and also a harijan, a member of the low-caste community that made up less than a quarter of the village population of 3,000. The water tank, the sole source for the village, was positioned in the high-caste, wealthier end of the village, and many of them had piped connections to their homes. As a result there was often little water available for the harijan community, the poorer people of the village.

Mr Chandrasekar had been one of the harijans who had taken their case to the local authorities, who had eventually decreed that the private water supplies to the high-caste Hindus should be disconnected and all water drawn equally from a tank in the centre of the village. It was to have ten taps: eight for the high-caste villagers, two for the harijans.

This was not a universally popular ruling, and the tank became the focus of tension between the two communities, as the high-caste villagers objected to drawing water when the harijans were present. Six months before our visit the situation had come to a head, when the harijans were prevented from obtaining water at all. Lily's husband had gone to the high-caste village leaders to protest.

At this point, our interpreter explained, the story became confused. The police had intervened and arrested him, taking him to the police station. It was while he was being questioned that he had been beaten to death. Some claimed that high-caste villagers had taken the law into their own hands, killed him and then ensured there would be no backlash from the harijans by setting fire to forty-five of their houses and two school buildings.

As we listened to the story, and looked at the photograph, it seemed almost unreal. A Christian school teacher, about my age, beaten to death because of water. But Lily's face was real. She explained that every night her three-year-old Noel, asked when Daddy would be coming home.

EFICOR had heard the story. They had sent the drilling-rig into Vilapakkam. They had gone straight to the heart of the harijan area, drilled down to sixty metres, and had hit water. But within weeks the supply had begun to dry up. The harijans were in despair. Having been set free from dependence on their oppressors, now they were to be forced to go back to them and beg for water. They were desperate. They were pleading for the rig to return and try again, and set them free. Now we began to understand the looks as we had driven in through the high-caste part of the village. EFICOR's drilling-rig could tilt the balance of power in the village. We had been allowed a glimpse of a spiritual battle, a battle for justice.

At that moment a man appeared asking for help. Would one of us please come and officiate at his opening ceremony? We were obviously the nearest he could find to a celebrity. Garth decided it was another job for 'staff', so I found myself being handed a pair of scissors, cutting the ribbon across the entrance, and declaring the bicycle shop open. It was no more than a grass hut, and his stock consisted of three Hero bicycles, carefully decorated with leaves from the nearby bush. It wasn't much, but he was as proud as Jack Cohen opening his first Tesco's.

As we returned to Vellore, then by train to Bangalore and plane to Delhi and on to Heathrow, we realised why *The Road to Freedom* was an appropriate title for the presentation. Rehousing flood victims on land provided free by the government broke the grip of the local landlords. Drilling a well was about more than just a glass of clean water. It could bring freedom and break shackles. Whether there was too much water or too little water, something could be done that did more than just scratch the surface of the problem of poverty.

We got home after an eight-day trip that had seemed like a lifetime of experience. Shortly after, I received a letter from the EFICOR drilling-rig team. They had returned to the harijan community in Vilapakkam, and they had hit water again, and this time the supply looked plentiful and secure. I still remember one phrase in that letter: 'the people's joy knew no bounds.'

8

Television Pictures

The images played and replayed in my mind . . .
There was something terrible about the idea that
* 2000 years after Christ,*
something like this could be allowed to happen.
Bob Geldof

The Road to Freedom was well received, from Dublin to Edinburgh. Thousands came to the event, and many expressed appreciation of the insights they received into the nature of poverty and the work of Tearfund. I enjoyed my foray into the world of gigs and touring, with its curious hours and adrenalin rhythms. Going to bed late and getting up late I was used to from my student days; the focus on being on top form for the evening performance, and not really being able to eat until midnight, was definitely stranger. It was part of the edge to the whole feeling of being on the road, living life to a different pattern. And the communication was powerful and positive; it helped to personalise the relationships with Tearfund's supporters.

So eighteen months later we found ourselves doing it again. A cut-down, simple version, delivered at the request of our Wales co-ordinator, designed to enable a quality event to reach some of the parts not usually reached. The audiences varied from small to medium, the Welsh scenery was wonderful – and something else happened. As we went through the week, Garth and I had more and more people coming up to us asking if we had seen the pictures. Some of them were clearly shocked, almost traumatised – and we did not really have much clue what they were talking about.

Each night when the six o'clock news came on, we were in a church hall setting up and getting ready for the evening performance. When the nine o'clock news came on we were in full flow. And by the time we had cleared up we had missed the ten o'clock news. There was no satellite, no cable. So we had not seen the pictures.

The pictures were from Ethiopia. They were accompanied by Michael Buerk's sombre reports on what he described memorably as 'a famine of biblical proportions'. It was the pictures that persuaded the news editors to tell the story at all. It was the pictures that provoked a fiery fading Irish rock-star to action and turned him into a saint with a knighthood. It was the pictures that shaped the attitudes of a nation and a generation. It was the pictures that gave Ethiopia its lasting one-dimensional image. And in two days' time I was going to Ethiopia.

The night before I left was Guy Fawkes night. As usual, we went as a family to the girls' school bonfire party. The rockets whooshed, the bangers banged, the sparklers sparkled. I tucked into the hot dogs with relish, literally and metaphorically. It was wonderfully English, cold and damp and lots of fun. The next day I was catching a plane to a land with a famine; some of those there that night wondered if I was taking food so that I would have something to eat myself.

The visit had been planned for some time. Since I had been twice to Asia, it was thought appropriate that my refresher trip after two years should be to Africa. John Capon, recently arrived to edit *Tear Times* and generally oversee Tearfund's publications, was going to Ethiopia, and it was agreed that I should join him, along with Tony Neeves and Graham Fairbairn, another long-standing staff member. Part of the reason for choosing Ethiopia as a destination was that Tearfund, along with the rest of the world, had been alerted to the impending disaster a few months earlier, and had already begun to respond. But now 470 million people had seen the pictures on 425 television stations around the world. None of us had expected to be flying to a country so recently catapulted to the centre of global attention. I am not sure any of us quite knew what to expect.

We left Heathrow in torrential rain, en route to our drought-stricken destination. As soon as we arrived, we were forced to make the one-dimensional view rather more multi-faceted. Here was a country with a Marxist revolutionary government attempting to operate a commercial economy. So on the short drive from the airport we saw no starving people; we saw giant adverts for whisky, we saw large banners with revolutionary slogans including the word 'proletariat', and we saw the tourist board posters encouraging foreign visitors with the slightly ironic slogan 'Thirteen months of sunshine', the result of Ethiopia's attachment to the Julian calendar.

We were met at the airport by a missionary with SIM (Society of International Ministries), the main evangelical mission agency in Ethiopia, and taken to their headquarters, where we quickly began to understand another unreported facet of the country. There were probably more evangelical Christians in Ethiopia than there were in Britain. About three million people belonged to the largest denomination, the Kale Heywet (Word of Life) Church. This was the church linked to SIM, and Tearfund was linked to them both – it was complicated, and clearly a source of some tension, but the fact remained that this Marxist country was still home to a group of foreign missionaries and a large indigenous church.

The next day, as we waited for our papers to come through so that we could travel outside Addis Ababa, we were able to meet Dr Mulato Baffa, the head of the Kale Heywet Church, and get a picture of Christians under pressure. Around fifteen hundred churches, more than half, had been closed by government decree, and about two hundred individuals were in prison. It was quite difficult to take in. Everything appeared so normal.

Addis itself seemed to be ticking over. There was none of the frantic bustle of Asia. Heavily laden donkeys and women walked past in a stately kind of way. The Shell petrol station just behind SIM headquarters carried the familiar logo, and I calculated that the price was familiar as well. Our guided tour of the city included Bingham Academy, formerly for missionary kids, now a school for diplomats' children, but still run by SIM. It was interesting to think that a Hungarian diplomat to a fellow-Communist state would have his children taught Bible verses by an American missionary.

We saw the lions as we went past the zoo, looking slightly mangier than perhaps they had been when cared for by the Lion of the Tribe of Judah, Emperor Haile Selasse. We saw an ITN camera crew in the Hilton Hotel, no doubt part of the media maelstrom that had descended on Ethiopia, and no doubt among those consuming some of the whisky imports that had so excited their media colleagues back home. We saw a few beggars, and a bread queue, but nothing to indicate that this was a country in major crisis, with two million facing starvation.

We were due to fly to Asmara, the capital of Eritrea, the northern province of the country, fighting for its independence. The travel permits came through just in time, and so did our very own personal security detail. She was obviously well-to-do, very quickly producing her photo album complete with family holiday snaps from Los Angeles. She told us she was a Christian, but it was difficult to know how to respond as we had no idea what she should know or should not know about us and our hosts. She told us to call her Jimmy, which only added to the confusion.

I settled into my aisle seat on the Ethiopian Airlines plane and fastened my seat-belt. The passenger next to me seemed to be having some difficulty with this task, so the stewardess leaned over me to offer assistance. This resulted in a very close encounter with a bare breast, which seemed to be escaping from its clothing about three inches from my nose. I was still trying to recover when the plane roared down the runway for take-off, an event which prompted an old Ethiopian gentlemen sitting a couple of rows in front to get to his feet.

The stewardess came running down the plane as it launched itself upwards, loudly berating the man for his refusal to obey instructions. When she realised why he had stood up, she was even more furious with him. There was something dripping from the overhead locker. The angle of the plane was now such that whatever the substance was, it was being spread rapidly, a steady stream flowing back down the line of lockers, dripping on to the passengers below at erratic but frequent intervals. They, of course, being law-abiding, were securely belted in, right in the line of fire.

Jimmy explained that the old man had carefully placed his pot of a traditional Ethiopian delicacy, a mixture of rancid melted butter and herbs, in the overhead locker, but apparently without realising that the plane would not always be level and at a standstill. So his pot had no lid. The pungent aroma filled the cabin, as stricken passengers attempted vainly to remove the smelly, sticky, fatty stain that had appeared on their shoulders.

We landed in Asmara. Ethiopia is the one African country never subjected to European empire, except for Eritrea, which was taken over briefly by the Italians. The legacy, according to one Eritrean we met, was wide roads and spaghetti factories. Asmara was certainly a delightful city, a lovely mix of Italy and Africa, with wide streets and pavements, all lit by a glowing sunset before the curfew came into force.

The next day we set off early in the VW combi. It was only a short distance in miles, but a long way in time and experience. There were a number of roadblocks, the soldiers usually uninterested and relaxed, although festooned with rifles and machine guns. There were a couple of burned out tanks on the road, just to remind us that the fighting had been for real. The countryside looked right for it. It reminded me of the setting for a spaghetti western, all barren bare rock and sand, hardly a trace of green in sight. The road wound down the valley, with high plateau in the distance, outcrops of hill sometimes topped by a village or a single Coptic church.

It looked inhospitable and infertile, but there had been some kind of crop because every now and then the road would be covered in grain, neatly spread out over the tarmac. This has now become a familiar sight in many countries, but I have to confess that in my Birmingham city-dweller ignorance I still have no idea whether this is to dry the grain or to wait for vehicles to drive over it to crush it. I can hear the chortles of the knowledgeable even now. I was just glad I wasn't driving, otherwise the answer to the question might have been important.

We reached our destination, Decamhare, a small town where Tearfund was supporting an orphanage attached to a church run by Pastor Michael. We turned in through the gates of the compound, and were engulfed by excited children, who got noisier and more boisterous by the minute. 'Hello,' they shouted, with grins splitting their faces from car to ear.

Their energy and movement was in sharp contrast to a group of adults sitting and squatting in the sun, hardly moving, hardly talking. They had come into the compound that morning, and were awaiting the food distribution they had been promised, which had been organised on this particular day at this particular time for our benefit. So when Tony was ready with his camera, the distribution could begin.

My task was to collect the stories to go with the pictures. Tony selected a couple of the group, which numbered about a hundred, and I began to interview them through an interpreter. The first was Hailu Hailom, a man whose sunken empty eye sockets indicated his blindness. His son held his hand as he explained that he was fifty-six-years-old and had been blind from birth. They had walked together 120 miles to find food.

Then I spoke to Tiekle. She was noticeable in the crowd because she was carrying a baby that had an enormous pink square Elastoplast on its forehead. Tiekle was twenty. She told briefly how she had walked 250 miles carrying her baby in search of food. It had taken her a week, and she had kept going by eating leaves and berries from the side of the road. Then I asked her how she had come to take the decision to set off on this journey. She explained that she and her husband had been unable to harvest any crops for three years, three years of drought. The cows and sheep had gone, the vegetables had run out. Finally they had nothing left except the seed grain for next year's planting. Once they had eaten that, their future had gone.

So one morning they had woken up, then made the decision that they would go in opposite directions, in the hope that one of them might find food. I asked her whether she ever expected to see her husband again. As she slowly shook her head, tears filling her eyes, I had an overwhelming sense of tragedy. For me it was finally an encounter with the reality of famine. In Britain, it had been the numbers, two million, that had seemed so monstrous; now it was the experience, the destruction of relationships with both home and family, the despair. It was not just two million: it was two million people, two million individuals, two million human beings, and every one with their own story, their own tragedy, their own despair.

I felt I had pried enough, asked enough questions. There was an awkward silence, then I asked the interpreter to express my thanks to her for answering my questions. I felt awkward, that I had exploited my position to get the story. I think I thought of assuring her of my prayers, but at that moment it seemed rather patronising and inadequate. As he passed on my thanks, I realised Tiekle had responded, and I asked him what she had said. 'We thank God for the help you have brought,' was the answer. I was glad she was not thanking me. I reflected that the Apostle Paul knew what he was talking about when he wrote his famine relief appeal letter to the church in Corinth: *'This service that you perform is not only supplying the needs of God's people but is also overflowing in many expressions of thanks to God'* (2 Corinthians 9:12).

The church insisted on feeding us before we left, and they led us into the simple church building where an enormous mound of spaghetti had been prepared, accompanied by a relatively small amount of sauce and some meat that gave the word 'chew' a whole new sense of intensity. But it was an important part of the visit, sharing the meal, expressing fellowship. Here was a church that had seen the rebels come and go, that was caring for orphans of war, and was now a source of food for hundreds who had walked for days in search of help.

As I was talking to Pastor Michael, I suddenly had the idea that it would be interesting to ask him why. 'Some people would say that as a pastor, your job is to look after people's spiritual needs. Why have you got involved in these other activities?' I said, and he immediately replied, 'I simply could not stand by and watch people suffer.' It was the authentic voice of a follower of Jesus. The debate about evangelism and social action is an academic discussion that is neither informed by love nor challenged by experience. Michael was simply echoing the biblical reality: *'If anyone of you has material possessions and sees a brother or sister in need but has no pity on them, how can the love of God be in you?'* (1 John 3:17, NIV Inclusive edition.)

That's why when people have said to me how awful it must be to meet the poor and enter into their experience, part of the answer is that I always meet them in the company of Christians active in care and compassion. I am not surprised by pain and suffering; but I am not only surprised but also encouraged and inspired by those who give themselves in service to the needy. It is that perspective that makes all the difference.

Pastor Michael and his fellow church members in Eritrea had every excuse. The need was overwhelming, they were low in numbers, they were under pressure from the authorities. But they could not stand by . . . Back in Asmara, I heard a little more about the pressure. We were introduced to the widow of the previous pastor in Asmara itself. Her eyes filled with tears as she explained that he had suffered from heart problems and had died leaving her with six children to support. I noticed his Bible college diploma neatly framed and hanging on the wall. It was from Moorlands College, a place I have often visited down in Dorset.

Daniel had taken over his pastoral responsibilities at Asmara. Like Michael he was reluctant to talk in front of Jimmy the security lady, and in fact he only really opened up in our hotel room, when he was sure he could not be overheard. Even then his eyes carried a slightly wary, almost hunted look. He had been arrested for attending church in his air force uniform. 'The best thing about being in prison,' he said, in an interesting choice of words, 'was that I had the chance to talk to hundreds of people about Jesus that I would not have otherwise met.' It was from others that I discovered the price he paid for this determined enthusiasm was spending two years of his three year sentence in solitary confinement.

Late that afternoon we visited a Coptic Orthodox church. There was a compound wall, then inside the main building there was another building, a bit like a holy of holies. The whole place made me think of a biblical synagogue; perhaps it was the beggar at the gate. I wondered how my faith and behaviour might be affected if I passed a beggar every time I went in or out of church. There was a solemn hush inside, broken only by the sound of the Bible being read: apparently part of the priestly duty was to ensure that the Word of God could always be heard in the church. Scenes from the lives of the martyrs were painted round the walls, in a naive style, brightly coloured – especially the one of the man being flayed to death, to my eyes more gruesome than inspiring.

We returned to our hotel, where a small group were gathered around a television, watching the Ethiopian equivalent of the six o'clock news. There seemed to be interminable pictures of African leaders arriving at Addis Ababa airport for a meeting at the headquarters of the Organisation of African Unity. The plane landed, the red carpet was rolled out, the soldiers saluted. Apparently you could judge the standing of each leader and nation by the length of time the camera lingered over their arrival.

Things became altogether more interesting when it became clear that international news was simply bought in from other countries – there was a BBC report from Nicaragua, then, even more intriguing, the presenter announced that in Britain striking miners were using guns in their battles with police. It was hard to believe that the situation had escalated so rapidly: in the BBC report that followed nothing was said about guns, although there was a mention of slingshot. The Ethiopians present pointed at the screen and made some animated comments. I found myself with an overwhelming desire to explain there was more to Britain than the miners' strike, a desire quickly stifled when an ITN report from Ethiopia came on to the screen. The one-dimensional view of Ethiopia seen in Britain had quickly followed the one-dimensional view of Britain seen in the rest of the world. It is always so much easier to reinforce stereotypes. But I had finally seen the pictures.

9

The Sheep and the Goats

The King will answer, 'Whatever you did for one of the least of these . . . you did for me.'

Matthew 25:40

The next morning we once again saw the reality. Asmara was not at the centre of the famine crisis, but there were still large numbers who had arrived in search of food, and the church, officially banned from meeting for worship, was an official agent for food distribution. The sacks of grain were stored in a room in the corner of the church compound, and all around the wall, standing in the shade, there was a queue of people, waiting to receive their ration. They seemed the epitome of patience, stoic and silent. Suddenly there was an unexpected commotion. The people in the queue surged forward, fighting to get into the doorway of the food store. The official guards, provided by the local authority, advanced with their batons raised and forced them back.

It was all over in a few seconds. We gathered that those at the front of the queue had received their ration, then, unaware of another room filled with grain sacks, reported to those still waiting that stocks were running low. The change of demeanour was dramatic, dignity overwhelmed by desperation. This was life on the edge. Women were in tears, one boy had a cut head. Then I noticed someone else was in tears. It was Jimmy. She had been talking to some of the women in the queue; perhaps it was only our visit that had brought to her attention the realities of her own people's plight.

The tiny church in Asmara, meeting secretly in a room in the Orthodox cathedral, its pastor dead and his successor only recently released from jail, was handling not only a relief programme but also a major long-term development effort in the area around the town. We drove out a short distance to Adi Abieto. The village was in the distance, but close by was a dam, holding back a reservoir filled with enough water to last a year. Close to that was a well topped with two pumps, surrounded by a small area of green which contrasted starkly with the dominant browny-yellow. Children were walking donkeys to the pumps and filling the leather water panniers over their backs. The village leaders spoke enthusiastically of the impact of the whole scheme.

The pumps were of a slightly different construction to the ones I had seen in India. They were called Boswell pumps, designed by Bruce Boswell, an engineer who in his early retirement had become a Tearfund overseas worker. His design was regarded as the best available in Ethiopia, manufactured in the country, ordered by government and UN agencies alike, and in use in hundreds of villages. What a great way to be remembered, your name attached to a high quality product that makes such a difference to the lives of ordinary people!

This was a scheme the church had made earlier. We tried to make it to the site of another village where a similar initiative was planned, but the vehicle broke down. The village was called Tselot, which apparently meant 'prayer'. I loved the idea of a church providing clean and living water in a place called prayer.

Saturday night in Asmara revealed another unguessed facet of life in Ethiopia. We were just on our way up to bed in the hotel when the lobby filled with teenage girls dressed in a remarkably personal interpretation of Western fashion. The day had been hot, and with the temperature still up in the eighties woolly and stripy leg-warmers gave a whole new meaning to the concept of fashion victim. At that moment we were unsure of the exact purpose of their visit. We soon found out. In fact, we were not really able to forget. Our rooms were on the fifth floor; the top floor, one floor higher, was the location of the disco. It was loud, it was cooking, it was throbbing.

Our alarm went at 4.30 a.m., superfluous and only just audible above the deep bass on high. We staggered down for a bleary breakfast, and were nearly mown down by the teenybopper exodus. This was the sunset to sunrise curfew disco – over at dawn, when it was safe and permissible to leave. War and famine cannot stem the onslaught of global youth culture.

Back in Addis, the bureaucratic security system meant that we could not head south straight away, so we were able to go to church instead. The International Evangelical Church was packed with over five hundred people for its second service of the morning. They announced that the following week there would be a special famine relief collection. In the evening we had supper with some of the leaders of the Baptists in Ethiopia. 'We know,' one of them said, 'that many people in Britain are giving generously to help us. Please tell them that we are praying for them.' Once again, they had authenticated the words of the Apostle Paul: '*And in their prayers for you their hearts will go out to you*' (2 Corinthians 9:14).

South to Soddo. We were on the Ethiopian road again. I say 'the' advisedly, because at the time Ethiopia did only have one road. It ran north-south the entire length of the country. Asmara to Decemhare was part of its northern incarnation. It was the road that shaped the Ethiopian famine. The starving people knew that if supplies were to come, the lorries would have to use the road. So they walked to the road. It was the towns along the road that had gathered the enormous numbers that had made the TV pictures so dramatic.

The road was interesting to begin with, revealing a little of life in the countryside. But as the day wore on, it became more monotonous, only for excitement to return with the darkness. I was sitting in the front next to our American missionary driver, who was determined to make up for the time we had lost waiting for our security papers that morning. For much of the journey I was only half concentrating, vaguely taking in that being the only road meant that it was used by occasional buses, lorries and more noticeably, flocks of animals.

The flocks were quite entertaining. They were usually flocks of goats. We would approach them at around 50 m.p.h., sounding the horn insistently. With the languor that can only be achieved by animals whose every expression and body movement communicates, 'I will move, but in my own time, and because I want to, not because you want me to,' they would sedately move out of the way. Usually. Sometimes we got quite close before they moved. Sometimes they moved suddenly and rapidly, as if they had finally taken in that the noise was coming from something big and fast and potentially painful.

That was when I asked how serious it could be if we actually hit one. Apparently very serious. Compensation would have to be agreed and paid on the spot. Things could get nasty. So I began to watch the flocks of goats with more interest. As it became dark, they were picked out in the headlights, and still seemed to react in the same variety of ways. Suddenly the man from Birmingham noticed something else. As the scattered flocks passed to make way for the speeding van, I seemed to detect that although all the animals were basically black and brown goat-like creatures, there did seem to be variations. I cleared my throat nervously, afraid at revealing my ignorance. 'Are these animals all goats?' I enquired. There was a chuckle. 'No, some are sheep and some are goats.' I believed him. Just because all the sheep I had ever seen were large white round woolly things. What did I know?

I watched for another hour. I still wasn't sure I could tell the difference. I tried to expand my knowledge further without giving away more of my ignorance. 'As you approach them,' I asked rather hesitantly, 'does it make any difference whether they are sheep or goats?' This turned out to be the key question. Apparently it made all the difference. Some of the flocks were entirely sheep, some entirely goats. Sheep and goats reacted differently to the horn. The goats tended to scatter, the sheep to wait for a leader to indicate the appropriate course of action, whom they would then follow. And when the flock was mixed, as many were, it was very difficult to predict which animal's reaction would dominate.

Suddenly a Bible story took on a whole new significance. In Matthew 25 Jesus talked about the Son of Man coming as King and separating the sheep from the goats. And the basis of that separation was not to be how they looked, but by how they responded to the stimulus of seeing someone in need. '*I was hungry, and you gave . . . I was hungry and you gave me nothing . . . Whatever you did for one of the least, you did for me . . .*' It was their reactions that revealed their nature. For sheep and goats read human beings. For the car horn substitute the needy. Our reactions will reveal our nature. We cannot become a Christian by feeding the hungry; but neither can we claim to be a child of God, and then ignore the cry of the poor.

In the Palestine of the time of Christ, so in the Ethiopia of today: mixed flocks of sheep and goats looking very much like one another were a common sight. A Bible story set in its context had come alive. It has been a recurrent experience. If the Bible is a Third World book, then if you want to get close to its world and closer to its truth, a visit to Ethiopia might do more than a 'pilgrimage' to the Holy Land. I had seen camels in Decemhare, a thorn-bush sheep-fold on the road to Asmara, the beggar at the gate at the Coptic church, families who had abandoned their homes in search of food, people thrown in jail for their faith, and now the sheep and the goats. It was like visiting an illustrated Bible.

* * *

In the south of Ethiopia, where the Kale Heywet Church was strongest, the famine was not so severe. There was still a threat, however. The hills around Durami were green, a sort of Lake District with African huts. But the farmer told the story. He stood in his field, showing me his maize crop. The stalks were tall, but the cobs were shrivelled. He shrugged his shoulders. Our guide was more animated. 'People back home in the US want to know why the poor don't make more effort,' he said. 'I've watched this man this year. He has put in hours of back-breaking work – and now he has nothing to show for it.' His voice tailed off, as if he was almost surprised by his own vehemence.

The story was revealing. In this part of Ethiopia they expect two periods of rain – the short rains and the long rains. The farmers wait for the rain to come, and when it starts, and softens the ground, they plough and plant their seed. This year rain had come early. Was it the start of the short rainy season? He had planted some of his seed, hedging his bets. He had lost. The rain had only lasted a week. The seed had sprouted, shot up and then been withered by the hot sun. No crop.

The date for the start of the short rains came and went. No rain. After a few weeks it started again. This must be it. A good proportion of the remaining seed went into the ground. It rained for a week. The seed sprouted, shot up, and was then withered by the sun. No crop. The time came for the long rains. The time passed. Then the rain started again. This was the last chance. He ploughed again. All the remaining seed went in. The rain lasted a week. The seed sprouted, shot up, and was then withered by the hot sun. No crop. Nothing. Except some stalks he could feed to the cows. The cows had more food than the people. The Third World peasant farmer is knowledgeable, resourceful, hard-working – and vulnerable.

Down at Kolshobo Tearfund nurses Ruth Cordle and Nikki Sullivan were hard at work, weighing and measuring babies. The weighing was particularly spectacular. A scale was hanging from a hook fixed to the lintel of the doorway of the simple hut. Under the scale there was another hook, from which some straps were suspended. The babies and children were fitted into these straps and then suspended from the hook. They did not like it. Ear-splitting screams rent the air. I carefully recorded the sound, and offered a line of Alan Whicker-style commentary: 'And here in deepest Ethiopia, Tearfund nurses are torturing children.' How we all laughed.

Actually, the heat and the screams brought on a rapid head-ache, and I was deeply impressed at the professional perseverance of the two nurses, who also had to cope with the attentions of children who stared with fascination at their every move. I discovered that one of the character-building aspects of overseas work is the difficulty of privacy, of being constantly watched, of having skin pinched, of feeling conspicuous. I also discovered the value of basic simple healthcare: weighing and measuring, and thus identifying immediate need, and organising supple-mentary feeding programmes.

In this area no one was starving, but malnutrition was widespread. The scenes were not as dramatic as the TV pictures, but that was partly because prevention was proving better than cure. Children at risk were identified. Food rations were available. The records showed significant improvements. The next day we visited the nurses again, at a nearby village called Gafata. The supplementary feeding programme was in full swing. Children clutching their brightly coloured plastic bowls queued up for their porridge, others drank milk from brightly coloured plastic mugs. They had little clothing but big smiles.

There were tears at our next stop. It was at Anka Wocha, a desolate and barren place, another base for the SIM/church operation in which Tearfund was involved. Here there was a food store, in a church building that had been re-opened so that it could be used for this purpose. On the door was pinned a hand-written notice, forbidding the use of the building for worship, by order. It did not look very official, but the signature obviously carried weight. The local government representative did not like the church, so he closed it. It was as simple as that.

I stood by the simple lectern. Nearby there was another hand-written notice pinned up. This one was the Lord's Prayer. 'Give us today our daily bread.' That was when I noticed that one of the young women assisting the food distribution was in tears. Had we upset her? Had we said the wrong thing? No; she was remembering how she used to participate in worship in this building, and was crying for the opportunities that had been missed, and the fellowship she had been denied.

There was at least evidence of a different kind of fellowship – the fellowship revealed by individuals and churches giving to Tearfund, who channel funds and skills to local Christians, who use them to make a genuine difference to needy people. We saw a spring that had been 'capped': a simple concrete platform topped by a pump, that meant clean water from the spout rather than drawn from a pond shared by the cows. We saw a thin plastic pipe. It did not look that exciting, but it was exciting enough for the people to whom it supplied clean water from over ten kilometres away.

At Anka Wocha I also achieved another first. We had passed hundreds of *tukuls*, African huts, but I had never been inside until now. It was midday, roasting hot. Since I was not a mad dog, I must have been an Englishman. Inside, it was cooler and, for several minutes, pitch black. I realised quite quickly I was sharing the small space, a circle of about six metres in diameter, with a number of animals. Apparently they were brought into the hut at night and at midday. They were of course the family's most valuable possession. As my eyes got used to the light I could see the furniture and interior decoration were definitely minimalist. I took a photograph. It was only when I looked at the slide when I got home that I discovered there had been a baby asleep in a hammock against the far wall.

At Ruth and Nikki's base they had prepared the staple Ethiopian meal of injera and wat, and we prepared ourselves for the experience. The injera was bread made from teff, the Ethiopian grain – but bread was an understatement. It was a giant, round, grey, spongy, tripe-like, sour-tasting, flat piece of dough, remarkable in that it achieved its bubbly texture by being allowed to ferment. And what was wat? The sauce, preferably with meat, that went on top of the injera.

The eating method was simple and direct. The diners sat round the injera in a circle. In went the fingers, which tore off a piece of injera, already absorbing the wat in a wonderfully squidgy way, and scooped up some more on the way to the mouth. It was a shared meal in every sense. We laughed, we dripped sauce down our beards (OK, one person did), we chatted, we extracted stringy chicken from our teeth, I was even paid the ultimate compliment, apparently, by being fed a mouthful by someone else. It was only later that we discovered the village had shared their last chicken.

On the way back to Addis we had one more visit. Daniel met us where the main road crossed the Bilate river. The river was no more than a trickle, dribbling through a minor canyon that looked a little like a lunar landscape. The trees had been cut for firewood, the soil had been washed away, bare rock exposed; the area was barren and apparently useless. But Daniel, an agriculture graduate from Addis Ababa University, was an enthusiast, and he was in the transformation business.

So he had persuaded the Marxist government to give the church 500 hectares of this wasteland, which was situated in a Muslim part of the country. The plan was to terrace the land, plant trees along the edge of each terrace to hold the soil, and see grazing return for the animals, fruit and firewood produced for the people. All the work would be done by the local people in exchange for food. Thus the benefits would be short and long term.

The work had just begun, and was being done at a tremendous pace, which we assumed may have been speeded up by Tony's camera. People were almost running with watering cans full of water. A cloud of dust rose from the group wielding hoes and spades, as they worked rhythmically, chanting loudly. There was the slight air of watching an old silent movie running at too high a speed. However fast, or slowly, they worked when unobserved, the fact was that the terracing was almost finished, and Daniel showed us the six-inch seedlings being planted along the edges. The transformation was under way.

He was full of vision – and realism. 'I want to see this whole area change and become productive. I want people to know that God is in the business of making the desert fruitful. But I'll wait until the trees are really growing before I put up a sign by the road that announces it is a church project!'

Three years later I bumped into Daniel in the Tearfund office. I was keen to discover how the project was going. 'You remember the six-inch seedlings,?' he asked. 'They are now about thirty feet tall. The animals are grazing on the terraces, it has all worked so well that the government has given us another 500 hectares of land on the other side of the river. Best of all, the local Muslims were puzzled as to why we had worked so hard in their area, and made sure they got the food for the work that needed doing, when we could have stayed in a Christian area. When we explained it was because we wanted them to know the love of God, they came asking us about our faith. And some of them have become Christians, even though it means they have had to leave their village.'

This was holistic mission at its best, motivated by love and embracing God's concerns for the land and the people, body, mind and spirit. It was inspiring, offering a vision of how the Christian gospel could be loved and lived rather than just talked about. Growing trees had been persuasive preaching. We so readily want to limit evangelism to a communication in words; it's relatively easy, it doesn't cost us a lot, and it is not very effective. When Tearfund was involved in a major environmental education and action initiative at the time of the Rio Earth Summit, I received a vitriolic letter asking why Tearfund was concerned to grow trees when people were heading for a lost eternity. The Bilate river project was a key part of my reply.

10

A Test of Faith

*In the West you have God and things;
here we just have God.*
                                        A Haitian pastor

It had been a good trip. We had seen first-hand some of the need;
we had seen what the Kale Heywet Church and SIM were doing
with Tearfund support. But John Capon, the professional journalist of the party, was acutely aware that we had not seen for
ourselves the Ethiopia currently appearing twice nightly on the
television news. His concern was that our experience might
appear to be peripheral when we returned, that some of the
authority gained by personal witness might be lost.

When we got to Addis and returned to the SIM guest house,
he was quick to get into conversation with the MAF (Mission
Aviation Fellowship) pilots who were also in residence. They were
flying north every day, calling in on the towns where the great
concentrations of famine victims were to be found. The flights
were sponsored by World Vision; journalists were being tran-
sported free – after all, it was their reports and pictures that were
filling the coffers as people responded with unprecedented
generosity.

We had a couple of days before we were due to fly on to
Kenya, so why not try for a day-trip to the famine? It seemed a
good idea at the time. So John and I tagged along with pilot

Keith, hoping that our papers might give us clearance, but somehow doubting it, and turned up to the airport trying nonchalantly to look as if we had every right to be there. And eventually, without anyone querying it, we took off. It was a small plane seating about fifteen. Up at the front was a soldier, rifle across his knees.

It was a spectacular flight: low over awesome mountains, valleys that looked like the Grand Canyon, catching a glimpse of little clusters of houses that seemed to be impossibly located at the top of cliffs, with no fences to prevent children and animals falling over the edge. And how did anyone get to them? 'Remote' seemed far too close a word to describe their location. Then the landscape became flatter and more barren. I caught glimpses of the road – yes, *the* road – winding its way north.

I had just noticed what seemed to be two lorries on the road, with smoke rising up from them, when the soldier leapt to his feet and the pilot suddenly threw the plane into a violent turn. While I tried to renew acquaintance with my stomach, which was still heading in the original direction, the soldier engaged in an animated discussion with the pilot. After a few minutes, the plane turned again, a little more sedately, and continued in the original direction.

Eventually we landed on a dirt airstrip, with the name 'Alamata' picked out in white stones so that approaching passengers could see exactly where they were arriving. We were collected by a World Vision vehicle and set off on the short ride into town. The road was busy with people on the same journey, some carrying firewood on their heads, although since there was not a tree in sight it was worrying to think how far they might have been walking with this precious cargo.

The town was even busier. The streets were crowded, and a large group of people were gathered on a square decorated with revolutionary banners and a battered portrait of Lenin. At the far end of town we discovered the World Vision feeding centre, very organised and with large numbers of people crowded into the compound. The neediest cases were being fed two basic porridge-style meals each day, and dry rations were also being distributed. It was not unlike what we had already seen, except in size. This was a big operation.

In one corner there was a building containing a number of rooms. It looked as if it might have been intended to be a school, but it rapidly became clear that this was the emergency hospital. It was staffed by some of Mother Teresa's Missionaries of Charity, and the nun who was the nursing sister in charge took us into one room after another, talking about their work with enormous enthusiasm. Her effervescence was in stark contrast with the desperate stillness of the patients. There were many in severe states of emaciation; there were many on drips, including tiny children with matchstick limbs; there were many unable to summon the energy to move their eyes to see the visitors; there were many who would not make it at all.

On the wall outside these small squares of desperation, I noticed a sign which read simply, 'No photos'. I asked the sister why she had made this ruling. She smiled, and said, 'God will make his own television pictures. He will record all that needs to be recorded.' It was a startling example of a rather touching, almost naive other-worldliness, in stark contrast to the pick-up truck that had scattered the crowd in the town, the TV cameraman standing in the back, the bulky camera on his shoulder. The Ethiopian famine was world news partly because you could get on the little plane, get off it two hours later, start shooting in seconds, catch the plane back the same afternoon and send the pictures off for transmission – all in less than twenty-four hours. The pictures make the news, and the ease and speed of obtaining them helps to decide which pictures make the news. But thank God not everyone's agenda is determined by the television cameras.

We walked through the town. It was quite a shock to realise that for the regular inhabitants of Alamata there was more to life than a famine. Schoolchildren went scurrying past, clutching exercise books. Apparently every child had a school place, and every child learnt English. We rapidly discovered what must have been the first lesson, as every child seemed to know just one sentence: 'Mister, give me pen.' There were very few variations. Occasionally we would be addressed as 'Brother', and even once as 'Sister'. But little changed in the rest of the sentence. I did wonder if they were asking for pence, but decided against this. It was amusing for fifteen minutes, then irritating, then disturbing. The famine that was in the process of killing perhaps two million of their fellow citizens had brought them a profusion of potential pen donors. It did not quite match up.

We had a Coke for lunch, then it was time to get the return flight to Addis. We returned to the airstrip. We waited. We gazed at the sky, playing the game of who will be the first to see the plane. There was no winner. The plane did not come. The driver began to get agitated. Suddenly we understood that he wanted to make sure he was back inside the town before the dusk curfew. We had little choice, and went with him. We were going to have to spend the night in Alamata.

He took us to what was called a hotel, where we checked in with all our luggage – a small camera bag each. The room was truly appalling. We weren't sure whether to be glad or sorry that there was still just enough light to see. The dirt levels were indescribable, but not more indescribable than the bathroom and the hole in the floor. We could hardly bring ourselves to look at the beds, let alone contemplate sleeping in them. I cannot recall ever being more grateful than when someone came down from the World Vision base and invited us to share their hospitality. We just hoped nothing had decided to leave the hotel with us.

Room 13 in the project building was small, but it was clean. There was about three inches between the two narrow beds, and about two feet to the wall either side, but since we had no luggage this was not an enormous problem. As it grew dark and we realised there was no electricity in Alamata, we enjoyed chatting to our hosts. Contrary to Western television assumptions, it was entirely an African team, mostly Ethiopian, all Christians, led by a Kenyan doctor who revealed that his biggest problem was persuading the helpers to stop to eat, emphasising to them that if they starved themselves, they would be no use to those already starving.

The American video crew arrived, viewing the day's work on a tiny four inch monitor. They had been in Korem, the site of Michael Buerk's original pictures. Their pictures were just as stark and powerful. 'These will keep the money rolling in,' commented one. I thought I could introduce him to the nun down the road; it would have been an interesting clash of cultures.

John and I decided it was time to turn in. There was one last thing to do. I scrounged some toilet paper and set off with a borrowed torch in the direction of the last room of the building. The door was a corrugated iron panel swinging wide on its hinges; inside was a concrete slab with a hole in the middle. The real problem was that the door had a piece of string tied to its handle, but there seemed to be nowhere to tie the string so as to keep the door shut.

Examination and thought revealed that there was a real dilemma. If I let go of the string the door would swing wide open, giving me a panoramic view of Alamata. I somehow felt that if I kept the torch on, it might give Alamata a panoramic view of me. If I switched the torch off, no one would know I was in there, but I would not know what else was in there with me. Neither could I put the toilet paper down, as the floor was rather wet. There was one positive to cling on to, literally: if I held on to the paper and the torch, then clutching the string to keep the door shut also prevented me from toppling over backwards. It's good to have a personal challenge from time to time.

* * *

Both of us woke early. It was still dark, but a strange dawn chorus seem to have begun. Some elements of it were instantly recognisable: cocks crowing in that slightly demented manner that suggests they will regard it as a personal affront if you do not wake up; sheep (or perhaps goats?) bleating plaintively; and was that a rifle shot we heard? But there was another element we could not recognise, a sound that added a strange and unnatural element to English ears.

As the first streaks of light began to appear, John decided to obey once again his journalistic imperative and get up and investigate. So at about 5.30 a.m. we began a walk down the main street we had driven up the day before. It was now packed on both sides with people; those who had been in the feeding station in the day simply bivouacked by the roadside for the night. There must have been thousands, closely packed. Some were in white, but most in grey or brown, giving an almost ghostly impression in the half-light, reinforced by the smoke from the few fires that had been lit.

We discovered the source of the unknown element of the Ethiopian dawn chorus. As we walked on we came upon the sight and sound of grief. The objects being wrapped in the white sheets were the bodies of those who had died in the night. The sound was the voices of the wailing of the relatives, traditional in its form and tone, agonising in its rawness and intensity. Famine victims die at night; the enfeebled bodies, starved of energy, succumb to hypothermia as the temperature drops towards freezing. On and on down the street the scene was repeated. It was unnerving. I felt I had intruded, an international observer at a private national wake. We had come to see; now we had heard.

We walked quietly back up to our hosts, and nibbled at breakfast while we talked over the national crisis – 'when elephants fight the grass gets trampled' – and our personal crisis. We discovered, not surprisingly, that the two were linked. The Tigrean People's Liberation Front's tactics in their independence struggle with Ethiopia included hit and run attacks on the road. The story began to piece together. The two lorries I had seen had been attacked and their load of grain set on fire; the driver of one lorry had been brought in with a bullet wound in the leg. (So it probably was gunfire we had heard in the night.) The soldier had seen the evidence of the attack, and ordered the pilot to turn back, fearing that the airstrip might have fallen into rebel hands – hence the dramatic stomach-churning manoeuvre. But the pilot had suggested checking that another plane was safe at Alamata, and so they had continued and dropped us off, only for all flights to be suspended when they shared their news on return to Addis.

We thought we should try and contact Addis and investigate our options. We went back down to the main street, which had now resumed its daytime persona. We ran the gauntlet of the 'Mister give me pen' lobby, and arrived, pinched and prodded, at the grandiloquently named Telecommunications Office. It was actually the one wind-up telephone for the whole town, and there was a queue of people waiting to use it. Perhaps 'attempt to use it' would be more accurate. There was a lot of conversation with the operator, and a lot of turning of the handle, but I am not sure anyone got through; we certainly did not.

I passed the day walking there and walking back and getting nowhere. Realisation dawned that we were stranded. We had no belongings, we had no ticket out, we had no means of making contact outside the town, there was occasional gunfire in the distance, it was hot; in fact, we were on our own. I was lent a radio and tuned into the BBC World Service, and discovered it was a Saturday: there was live commentary on Spurs v Ipswich from White Hart Lane. It was a voice from another planet. It was followed by the full football results. Birmingham City had lost to Charlton Athletic. I couldn't believe it.

I couldn't believe I couldn't believe it. All the emotion and frustration of the situation seemed to focus on this football result. I was sharing a town with thousands of starving people, and I was upset Birmingham had lost. I got irritable with myself, and I got irritable with John. I remembered Christians were supposed to trust God when things got tough, and I got even more irritable. I can now look back on twenty-four hours when all the usual props I rely on in life were removed – it was a test of faith, and I think I probably failed. But then it occurs to me that I had not had much in the way of 'mocks'. Those who are uncertain of the next meal, who have no insurance or welfare benefit system, who have no access to a doctor – they know rather more of what it means to live by faith; they get more practice.

Next morning, after a sleepless night, we decided we would catch the bus south, and risk the road. No sooner a decision than a catch – the bus was not going to run. We returned to the bar of the hotel we had been rescued from the first night, and began a few hours in the company of a group clearly auditioning for character parts in a Graham Greene novel. There was a Finnish Red Cross team, comprised of a Japanese doctor, an Irish nurse, a Korean, and a Finn, playing cards with a kind of manic intensity.

They were joined by the two English charity tourists, out in the midday sun with just a camera, and then later by a large bear-like American. He worked for the US aid agency CARE, and he had been to most of the world's trouble-spots over the past twenty years, and had an interesting discussion starter as to whether Vietnam was worse than Lebanon was worse than Bangladesh was worse than Cambodia was worse than Ethiopia. In the corner was a freelance French photographer, very Jean Paul, travelling with an equally French-looking *très chic* reporter for *Le Monde*. They were more than travelling together; they were entwined together as if joined at the hip, and they smoked their Gauloises with great patriotic intensity. He had one big question – were there more people dying further down the road? If so, he had to be there. Death was obviously the way he earned his living.

There was a noise of a plane. It flew low over Alamata. The

cards were collected rapidly, the assembled host piled into a vehicle to drive out to the airstrip, fighting the flow of people pouring into the town. The plane was going the wrong way, but its arrival suggested that salvation might be at hand. The card game resumed. Another plane was heard. Everyone scoured the sky, the cards lay forgotten. The plane landed; it had engine trouble. The cards were picked up again. Another plane – ours. We piled in. It was a bumpy flight back to Addis Ababa, but one thing I knew – there was a hot bath waiting when it was over.

We were back in time to catch our onward flight to Kenya. We had an intensive three-day trip seeing various Tearfund-supported projects: water-pipes, meals for children, agriculture, sewing machines. We also looked in on a game park or two, seeing various animals: lions, ostriches, giraffes, jackals, waterbuck. The scenery was spectacular, the countryside green after three weeks of rain. We ended the trip eating a banana picnic overlooking Lake Nakuru, shimmeringly pink with thousands of flamingoes.

Then it was up on to the highlands, 7,500 feet and bitterly cold, for a final project visit. Drought in the area had prompted an emergency feeding programme. Thirty women had come to receive their sacks of grain, but before they received them, they had to endure a Stephen Rand sermon. I was not at all sure this was a good idea, but our host assured me that as Christian women they would be offended and disappointed if they did not hear the Word of God preached before they went home.

The food distribution consisted of maize, fat and milk powder. They would have liked to have included beans, part of the local staple diet. But there were no beans available in Kenya, they simply could not be obtained. So after the sermon the ladies went home, and so did I. I was glad to be home. Susan welcomed me with a roast dinner which included, as a special treat, an ingredient new in Sainsbury's: Kenyan beans.

11

Guinea Pig for Lunch

What is food to one man may be fierce poison to others.
Lucretius

My overseas visits should surely do more than simply provide me with information, impressions, stories and pictures: I have no wish to be entirely selfish. I feel that my presence and interest should offer some encouragement, perhaps even inspiration, to those I meet, whether Tearfund overseas workers, national project leaders or those slightly awkwardly called 'beneficiaries'.

I am less sure that I fully appreciate achieving this by being treated as an object of merriment. I was suspicious from the moment that Steve Finamore first informed Jennifer and me that we were travelling by horseback that morning. My suspicions grew when the gaggle of slightly mangy, slightly uninterested-looking nags arrived outside our lodging, and I was allocated what appeared to me to be the smallest. Steve kept his face straight long enough to say 'The question is, what would be easier – the horse carrying Stephen, or Stephen carrying the horse?' before bursting into helpless laughter.

I did not think the joke was that funny. Neither was me sitting on horseback, surely. I may have been from Birmingham, I may never have ridden a horse before in my life, but I had seen a lot of Clint Eastwood westerns. I was game. The question was whether the horse was.

* * *

This was my first visit to Latin America. I was travelling with Jennifer Loughlin, our Director of Overseas Personnel, who was making visits to Tearfund workers across the continent. We had already travelled via Miami – my first visit to the USA, leaving the sanctuary of the air-conditioned airport for one minute – to Honduras, where the highlight had been visiting the remote Mosquito Coast region and facing a new version of the bedroom challenge.

I had been lying in bed writing my diary, safe under my mosquito net, the sound of the water of the lagoon lapping on to the beach ready to lull me to sleep, when I had seen the rat gazing at me balefully from a few feet away. That was when I remembered I had forgotten my torch, and that the light switch was three paces from the bed. Or did I realise the light switch was three paces from the bed, and then remember I had forgotten my torch? Whichever, there were other questions. How long does it take to walk three paces? How fast can a rat run? Do mosquito nets keep out rats? What else could get into the bed while I was getting in? It was *Mastermind*, special subject 'Sleeping Peacefully', and I was passing on far too many.

The irony was that it was the bed-bugs I should have worried about. By the time we arrived in Peru, via an overnight stopover on a Caribbean island – there was no other way, honest – my backside was doing an impression of teenage acne, just ready for a few hours in the saddle. Steve had met us at Lima airport, escorted us to our amazingly posh hotel, accompanied us to the Anglican church the following Sunday morning and to the Spanish-speaking Alliance church in the evening. Here, after an evangelistic service where around fifty had gone to the front in response to an appeal to commit their lives to Christ, we were followed out of the church by some enthusiastic young people who caught up with us at the bus-stop, keen to know why as visitors we had not gone forward and to assure us it was not too late to be saved.

There was a different religious experience the next day. In the middle of one grey shanty area, I caught sight of the word *Justicia* painted slogan-like on a door. Here was the authentic cry of the poor for justice; then I realised it was a Bible verse, Proverbs 14:34: 'Justicia exalta a la nación.' In English this is traditionally seen on fading posters on rotting railway stations as 'Righteousness exalteth a nation.' The Spanish sounds rather more radical, even though both are accurate translations of the Hebrew word, which simply means 'doing right'.

Steve was married to Becca, a nurse, and they were seconded to the Presbyterian Church of Peru, working up in the Andes and based in Cajamarca, where the Inca leader Atahualpa had been captured and killed by the Spanish Conquistadors. So after a few days in the damp, drizzling, dreary-grey Lima visiting what are technically known as revolving loan micro-enterprise projects, we had flown up to Cajamarca and joined another couple, Tearfund workers Michael and Sarah French.

Our initial exploration of their work included a visit to Jesus, a nearby small town that had been featured in a Tearfund filmstrip. The inevitable comments provoked by its name reminded me that the two rugby matches I had played for my Cambridge college had both, in a strange Faustian coincidence, been against Jesus, which had made the yells of encouragement and instruction from the touch-line particularly unhelpful.

So now I was sitting on a horse in Celendin, high in the Andes, and about to go higher. The only delay was while we waited for Steve to recover from his laughter. It was rewarding to know I could bring such joy into the lives of others. For two hours we climbed steadily and relatively straightforwardly, until on a plateau about 3,000 metres high we reached our destination. It was a small village, one of the places where a nurse was hard at work on a community health programme. Marie-Christine Lux was around five feet tall and a pocket-sized dynamo of enthusiastic energy. A Belgian national, born in Congo and with Scottish links, she had first worked with Tearfund in Somalia, and now she was bringing her forceful personality to bear on improving the health of the local Indian communities.

Our visit was expected. The local schoolchildren had gathered to welcome us, accompanied by lots of mums and a few dads. The presentations began with different classes singing their health songs. There was a competition to see who could write and perform the best, so we listened as one group after another performed their compositions with varying degrees of tunefulness. Some had drum accompaniment, some had Andes pan-pipe accompaniment, some had both. I was getting rudimentary translations, revealing that these children were belting out enthusiastically raucous renditions of songs about parasites and diarrhoea, which were considerably more direct, graphic and didactic than the understated English health song 'Ring a Ring of Roses'.

Then Marie-Christine went into action. It was a bravura performance. She was addressing the children on the vital topic of water and latrines. I think she was consciously using all her best child communication techniques knowing that mums and dads were listening. As all truly humble preachers know – or is it all really bad ones? – it is the children's talk that adults remember, and the adults who probably appreciate it most.

These adults seemed incredibly weather-beaten, no doubt the result of outdoor living at this altitude. They were wearing white hats, somewhere between a bowler and a trilby. Apparently each tribe of South American Indians has a distinctive design of hat, sometimes black, giving a solemn topping to their colourful woollen clothing. What was particularly wonderful here was to see tiny tots being breast-fed, their own miniature bowler safely in place. Did every home have a carefully size-graded supply of bowlers to ensure that every tot could always have a good fit? Or did the Celendin Mothercare have a special children's bowler section?

Some of the men were chewing coca leaves, adding little bits of white powder from small wooden pots on to the wad of leaves in their mouths. I was assured it was limestone. Marie-Christine was determined to make the most of their presence. The government were giving free concrete latrine bases to all those who dug their own pits. So having explained the importance of building and using a latrine, she paused and asked the fathers who had done the work to qualify for their concrete free gift. The children swivelled to look at them, ensuring maximum affirmation for those who had raised their hands, and maximum embarrassment for those who were now standing, head down and hands by their side. Then we all moved into the communal hall to view an exciting slide show about latrines. This was obviously the topic of the day. I should have been warned.

It was now lunch-time. We were taken over to a house where serious cooking must have been going on for some time. I was solemnly assured that local etiquette demanded that my plate should be cleared to avoid offence to my hosts. The plate I received was well filled. We sat down, with a glorious view of the mountains in the sunshine, and I set about the eating task with my usual gusto.

My usual gusto did not last long. It was a stew, and it was demanding in all sorts of respects. There were enormous bits of sweetcorn that were chewy and gritty; there was rice, there were potatoes; there was a recognisable chicken leg, with a little meat and a lot of sinew. There were lots of small bones, and some of them had stringy grey meat attached. I am not sure exactly when I discovered I was eating guinea pig, but it did not make my battle to clear the plate any easier.

I should have least have been grateful it was a stew – it was impossible to tell whether any particular piece of meat was chicken or guinea pig, and I have to confess my taste buds were not really up to the distinction. On a later visit to Lima, my companion ordered roast guinea pig in a restaurant, and it came whole, sort of sliced up the middle and flattened on the plate, a little leg pointing to each corner of the compass. I was at least spared that, except by proxy.

I knew that guinea pigs were part of the Andean Indian diet. In fact the only reason we have them available as pets is because they were bred for food in Peru. Tearfund had supported a guinea pig breeding programme, but we had decided not to publicise this in our children's publications. My experience confirmed the wisdom of that decision. When I returned home, and revealed to my daughters the full extent of my carnivorous activities, I could tell by their faces I had seriously damaged my standing in their eyes. Crackle, their prized pet guinea pig, took it more personally. Not long after, she began to show signs of distress, and despite, or perhaps because of, the best efforts of the vet, she passed on. She was placed in a shoe box and I solemnly buried her under the rose bush. I was guilty, and I was yet to be forgiven.

My plate of stew was fought to a standstill. Only then did I discover that my guides and mentors had been economical with the truth. They had come prepared with plastic bags stowed about their persons, so that when the meal became too much, there was a ready receptacle to be surreptitiously used to save face – and stomach.

After guinea pig for lunch, it was time to retrace our steps – back to Celendin, back to Cajamarca, and catch the early plane to Lima the next morning. The horses had either been given time off for good behaviour or their efforts had left them exhausted – whatever the reason, we descended on foot. In fact, for the rest of the day, it was downhill all the way.

We ended up in two distinct conversations and gender groups. Jennifer, former radiographer, and Becca, nurse, were deep in one conversation. Steve and I strode out ahead, engrossed in a debate about Spring Harvest and Greenbelt, worship and the merits of the Baptist Hymn Book and other vital topics of church life. It all made sense at the time. We had been walking for well over an hour when disaster struck. The conversation was so intense that as we rounded a corner I forgot to think carefully about where I was putting my feet, and suddenly I trod on the edge of the path, some loose stones gave way, and my foot twisted over.

I yelped in pain and collapsed to the ground, which was the cue for Steve to burst into peals of laughter in a moving display of deep pastoral concern. 'What we need to do,' he announced, 'is to pray that a radiographer and a nurse come round that corner.' Within seconds, Jennifer and Becca appeared. 'Lord, a miracle,' Steve bellowed, chuckling proudly at his instant wit. I was not laughing quite as much. I knew exactly what had happened, because a few weeks earlier I had done the same thing, and it had been diagnosed as a torn ligament in my foot.

As I sat on the ground feeling sorry for myself and lapping up the female sympathy and medical concern that was now overcoming the merriment, I remembered what had happened on that previous occasion. The initial pain had given way rapidly to a dull ache, and then the foot had swollen such that the slightest weight placed upon it resulted in an explosion of pain, making walking almost impossible for days. So I dragged myself up to my feet, knowing that if I did not set out straight away I might never make it. How far was Celendin? As I limped on my way, I hoped it was not too far. It wasn't. Very soon the countryside gave way to the mud houses on the edge of the town, and I entertained various of the townsfolk as I hobbled past them, looking forward to the relief of the vehicle for the next stage of the journey.

It was a journey that extended my education in a whole number of important areas. First, medical. Second, driving technique. Third, psychology. To place them all in context, we were travelling on an unmade road through the Andes, full of twists and turns and hairpin bends, occasionally with sheer drops of thousands of feet falling away from very close to the edge of the road. Just to add to the excitement, there were a few houses by the side of the road which usually announced their presence by the resident dog leaping at the car, barking furiously, and then chasing it, still barking, for some distance. And it was getting dark and beginning to rain. Before we were halfway back to Cajamarca, it was pitch black. It meant you could not see the drop, but neither could you see the dogs, who would suddenly launch themselves out of the darkness.

The medical discovery was painful. I had imagined that the car would enable me to take the weight off my foot. Wrong. Take it from me, when you are in the back seat of a twisting and turning car you do a surprising amount of bracing your body with your feet to cope with the movement. And when a barking dog suddenly appears at the window inches from your nose, you tend to press non-existent brakes in reaction. It was agony.

The lesson in driving technique emerged slowly. As it grew dark and there were a few drops of rain on the windscreen, the car would occasionally give a good impression of a sideways drift while going round corners. Steve, who was driving, said knowledgeably but slightly less reassuringly, 'The rain must be making the surface slippery.' He drove on for about thirty minutes, leaving us glad that we were in the hands of such an experienced driver in these conditions, who would undoubtedly not allow the slippery surface to defeat his ability to keep the car on the road. It was only when we stopped for a drink that we discovered the slippery road was the result of a flat tyre rather than the weather.

That was when I received new insights into psychology. I was unable to do anything to help to change the wheel; even putting my foot on the ground resulted in waves of pain. As a result, in a continent famous for *machismo*, I had to watch helplessly while the women assisted. I was not sure my security in my own masculinity would ever recover. The only advantage I could perceive in my plight was that the agony in my foot was preventing me from worrying about the dangers of the journey. Pain changes one's perspective on life very powerfully.

We arrived back in Cajamarca. It was about nine, but it felt like about two in the morning. I was desperate for sleep, but before I could crawl off to my bed I was greeted with great enthusiasm by the project director, who had been waiting for us to return so that he could get a full debrief on our views and impressions of the day. I managed about ten minutes of mumbled and incoherent conversation before he realised that I was not going to be of much help to him. I made it to bed. I fell asleep wondering if I would be able to make it to Paraguay and Argentina or whether I would have to return straight to London.

I woke up wondering if I would be able to make it ten metres down the corridor to the toilet. There was that awful realisation that the question was insistent and the answer could not be put off for long. The guinea pig's revenge! My foot debated the matter with my stomach, but not for long. It was a debate that was repeated several times during the rest of the night. My stomach won every time, even though my foot was insistent that it was most unhelpful to get the runs when you can't walk.

When the morning eventually arrived, I felt dreadful. Apparently I looked pretty dreadful as well. White as a sheet, delicate of stomach, unable to walk . . . and a plane to catch. Sarah French was wonderful, caring and considerate, encouraging me to move when the stillness of death had attractions. I refuse to believe she was solely motivated by the worry of how long she might have to nurse me if I did not catch the plane. I can remember sitting, or rather slumping, in the non-luxurious departure lounge of Cajamarca airport, trying not to wonder what the toilet facilities might be like. Sarah remembers it too; when I saw her again after her return home, she was interested to discover that deathly white was not my usual colour, and that I was, in fact, capable of movement.

Interestingly, Michael French is now an Anglican minister; Steve Finamore is a Baptist minister (and a member of the Tearfund Board). I like to think that perhaps I helped them see something of the challenges and opportunities of the pastoral ministry. Anyway, I made it to Lima. The plane was met by someone pushing a wheelchair, and I made about the most public entry possible to the arrival buildings. From there I made it to the hotel, and I slept and I recovered. My daughters, of course, knew that I deserved everything I got. Guinea pig for lunch, indeed.

12

Meeting the Enemy

Our enmities mortal, our friendships eternal.
                                                    Cicero

Paraguay – 'land of peace and progress' said the sign at the airport. Especially if you were a Nazi war criminal, I couldn't help thinking. At least my stomach was now at peace and my foot was making good progress. I was ready for anything. The intrepid Brummie was even ready to risk alien territory and do battle with the countryside again.

It turned out 'countryside' was rather a small and inadequate word. The Chaco is a vast inland plain, hundreds of miles across, that straddles Argentina and Paraguay and parts of Bolivia and Brazil. Once the extremely comfortable coach had left the smart new cars and buildings of Asuncion behind, it headed down the Trans-Chaco Highway in a steady straight line for four hours. The land was completely flat, with lots of trees and birds, but there was no cultivation, so no fields, so why bother with bends?

We were travelling with Tearfund nurse Jenny Fewings, and when we got off the coach there was another Tearfund worker to meet us, Nigel Poole. He drove us off into the sunset on a reasonably good non-tarmacked road, and after dark we entertained ourselves spotting wildlife in the headlight beam – nightjars, frogs, foxes and, best of all, an armadillo. After ninety

110

minutes we reached the mission base at Makthlawaiya, the nearest thing to a village for many a mile, and effectively an island in the middle of a swamp. Nigel's wife Alison greeted us with a lovely meal, and we began to discover some of the challenges and realities of life in the Chaco.

The area was very sparsely populated, small Indian clan communities scattered about, some of them almost nomadic, living by hunting and fishing. Anglican missionaries from SAMS (South American Mission Society) had reached the Chaco about a hundred years ago and had considerable success, so that the Anglican Church was now the main, possibly only, source of cohesion and organisation in the area. Makthlawaiya boasted a corrugated iron version of a parish church from the Sussex Weald, and I met a man working on translating a third version of the Bible in Lengua, a language spoken by about four thousand Indians, of whom only a small percentage were literate. He had what was then a new-fangled personal computer (I mean, we are talking the 1980s here!) which impressed me most when he decided to change the phonetic spelling of one sound: he only had to hit one key, and the spelling was changed in every word in which it occurred in the whole Bible – and all in micro-seconds.

The Chaco, and the traditional way of life of the Chaco Indians, was under threat. It was the Wild West all over again. The Indians had lived here since time immemorial, but of course they had no legal rights to the land so far as the settlers' law was concerned. And the land was suddenly in demand. Beef cattle could graze, get fat and fetch a good price in the market, given the insatiable global appetite for burgers. So ranchers bought the land, put up fences and made their money. They also destroyed the grazing – and the way of life of the Indians. What was the church to do?

They had adopted a two-pronged approach: fight for the land for the Indians, and help them adapt to the change that was assumed to be inevitable, as the right to roam for hunting and fishing was increasingly curtailed. In Argentina and in Paraguay various methods had been tried. In Paraguay land had been bought for the Indians, and La Herencia, the social arm of the church, had tried to turn the Indians into first farmers and now ranchers. If you can't beat them, join them. Nigel was a specialist cattle man, and the project was approaching a critical moment, as it planned to divide the herd of several hundred among the Indians rather than continue to own the cattle on their behalf. It was a controversial decision in a difficult battle with social change, and hours of discussion were still going on.

From Makthlawaiya we moved on a short distance to Sombrero Piri and met up with Chris and Alison Hawksbee, again with Tearfund, and deeply committed to the Chaco Indian people. Chris was due to take us to La Patria, one of the areas of land bought for the Indians. We set off up the Highway, then turned off and bumped our way along a dirt road, with lots of sightings of kingfishers and giagantic storks. Suddenly a little animal darted across the road in front of us. Elijio, an Indian employed by La Herencia, shouted from the back of the truck. Chris braked hard, and Elijio streaked off into the bush with his rifle. After a few seconds we heard a shot, and he returned holding aloft a raccoon, once again the triumphant hunter.

About noon, after numerous stops to open and close the gates that symbolised the problem, we arrived at the settlement. Chris took us off to meet one of the local ranchers, whose land bordered the Indians' land and had created a fencing problem. It was all highly polite and civilised; we were given a warm welcome and a delicious grapefruit drink, and it was hard to sort out exactly how I felt. Was he the enemy? Or just someone pursuing his living quite legally, but in a way which happened to threaten the traditional livelihoods of others? It happens in Britain, it happens all over the world. It would have been simpler if he had been unpleasant.

Late in the afternoon, Elijio lit a fire and I watched him

expertly skin and prepare the raccoon. We got our beds ready, wooden rectangles criss-crossed with strips of hide. Jenny showed us the murky pool where she collected her water, for this was her particular base in the Chaco. She also showed us her shower, a bucket suspended from the eaves of the house, complete with a rope to pull that tipped it over so the water poured out. The most significant feature of this arrangement was that it was outside the building. I decided that bright moonlight on my pale expanses might frighten the animals, and decided to pass on this one, at the same time once again reflecting on the awesome commitment of these overseas workers.

This was the countryside. Hundreds of miles from the nearest town, no electricity, no mod cons. We sat round the camp-fire and I sampled the barbecued raccoon. It was like being on safari in the Wild West. As the sun went down, parakeets squawked and flocked to roost in the line of grapefruit trees. There was a sound, a sort of deep clanging, clunking sound, and everyone started to move.

They were responding to the ringing of the church bell. About fifty metres through the trees we came upon the Anglican church. The church bell was a short piece of railway line hanging from a tree and being banged with a stick. (Railway line? Just where was the nearest railway line?) The roof was the clear night sky, with more stars than I had ever seen and the Milky Way revealed as if a paint-brush had daubed the heavens. The walls were the trees of the forest. At first I thought people were approaching with torches, then I realised that fire-flies were flickering through the trees. In short, I thought it was the most beautiful church I had ever seen. I still do. I have since stood in giant cathedrals and gazed in awe at the lofty pillars and the fan vaulting, then I have remembered that these are human attempts to replicate the Creator's woodwork.

But in the end the church is people. The small Indian community gathered, and sat on the log benches that were arranged two-deep in a simple square. Then the old Indian pastor, the first baby born in the settlement after the missionaries had built Makthlawaiya, way back in 1907, stood at the lectern – a branch set as a crossbar on two branch uprights – and flicked on a tiny Duracell battery torch to read the scripture. '*In my Father's house there are many mansions . . .*' he read from John 14. It seemed deeply appropriate.

If my very first encounter with Christians from another culture had been reassuringly familiar, this was breathtakingly, beautifully different and enriching – so different that the missionaries were concerned at the level of Indian understanding of the gospel, given their language was short of abstract words, words to describe concepts rather than things. So different that when they stood up to sing, the sound did not seem to conform to Western musical patterns at all. It seemed full of urgent and discordant passion; Graham Kendrick it was not.

It was a memorable evening. It was hot, so our beds were out on the veranda and we slept under the stars. When I woke at 6.00, it was to discover that a wild animal had been rooting through our luggage in the night, and that the weather had changed. The temperature seemed to have dropped about 20°C; the warm night had turned into a cold morning. I discovered why the Indians went everywhere with their ponchos, which were now wrapped tightly around them.

Chris turned up with horses. Previously never having ridden in my life, I was now to get my second chance in a couple of weeks. Jennifer got a very dopey horse, much to her annoyance. It would stop and eat the grass when it felt like it, regardless of her efforts to persuade it to move. Mine just plodded on, slow and steady. I wound Jennifer up by giving her equestrian advice in my most patronising tone, as if my relative success was in some way down to me. The highlight of the day was crossing a wide river. The horse plodded in; when the water reached the stirrups I took my feet out, deciding to risk falling off completely in the attempt to keep my feet dry. Jennifer's prayers went unanswered, and I made it safely to the other side.

We were accompanying Chris on his rounds. He would travel like this to visit the tiny communities within La Patria, ready to offer agricultural advice and general encouragement. He was not able to announce his coming – no telephones here. So we arrived at one location to find all the rudimentary homes deserted, everyone had gone off hunting. At others Chris and his guests were welcomed warmly; Chris would sit with them, sharing *tereré,* the customary drink. It was a kind of tea, thick with the leaves of various plants, and sucked through a metal or wooden straw with a strainer on the end, so that you could actually get the liquid. I had a sip; it was clearly an acquired taste, and, Chris assured us, very powerful, to the extent that he suffered withdrawal symptoms when he left the Chaco.

A drink and a conversation, then it was time to move on. That was apparently often the extent of the agriculturalist's work. Chris was convinced that where the community was strong in its Christian faith, then it was strong in every way. People worked together more effectively, produced more food, got on with the tasks that made for progress, and were receptive to the advice he could give. Their motivation came from their closeness to Christ, and therefore effective development was only possible within this spiritual framework. So fellowship, encouragement and prayer could achieve more than a bag of fertiliser or a new technique. Holistic mission took on a new dimension.

The day's horse-riding over, we left La Patria. It was dark when the truck reached the Highway, which was up a few feet on an embankment to protect it from flooding. Chris stopped, switched off the engine, ran up the bank and stood very still, listening intently. Then he ran back, jumped into the cab, started the engine and raced and bumped his way on to the tarmac. As we drove on in a slightly more normal manner, he explained that because the Highway was very straight it was regarded as an excellent race-track for the rich young men of Asuncion to give their Mercedes a good run out. The problem was that someone had started the rumour that driving without headlights saved the battery – so it was not unknown for black saloons to come hurtling down the road at 120 m.p.h., completely unlit. But they could be heard some distance away, hence the interesting 'How to join a major road' technique we had witnessed, not to be found in most Highway Codes.

We travelled back to Asuncion in the truck. Chris wanted to bring some of the Indians, partly to visit an agricultural exhibition, but also to give them some experience of the capital. He argued that if they were ever to take reponsibility for their own affairs, some of them would have to feel at home going to visit government offices to argue their case. It made for an entertaining journey. Twenty Indian men, all wrapped in their thick woollen ponchos, climbed into the back of the pick-up. There were four of us, and the cab seated three. Jenny Fewings, bless her, decided that as she was most acclimatised, she would join the open-air squash in the back for the four-hour trip. I don't know what it did for her comfort or her reputation, but the sight of the vehicle's arrival in Asuncion certainly stopped a fair few pedestrians in their tracks.

At the mission house, the Indians gratefully climbed out, made for the back garden, lit the fire, started on the *tereré* and tried to make themselves feel at home. They clearly felt as out of place in the city as I had sleeping under the stars out in the Chaco. I was back in a city. There was traffic and shops and cafés. A week on another planet was quite long enough for me.

Our final stop was to be Argentina. This was an interesting prospect, because although the Falklands conflict had been over some time, an official peace had not yet been agreed and technically Britain was still at war. Our visas had been obtained via the Swedish embassy, and there was just a twinge of nervousness when we were waiting our turn in the immigration queue at the airport and a voice boomed out, 'All British passport holders this way.' We turned out to have an official specially for us, so the net result was that we were through immigration and customs in record time – a slightly unexpected result of modern warfare.

Jennifer and I were met by Tearfund worker Sheila Dale, who had stayed on through the war, and even on the drive into the city from the airport I began to realise that if the city was my kind of environment, Buenos Aires was my kind of city – it was something else. The main streets were grand and wide, the streets were buzzing and the shops were open until 11.00 p.m.

They also eat meat. This is no place for vegetarians. There are enormous restaurants where ox roasts take place in the window, and truly horrendous-size platefuls of meat are served to enthusiastic diners. The speciality is the *parrillada*, a sort of carnivorous Full Monty, which enables you to sample the entire animal in one go: the steak, liver and kidney are accompanied by a sausage made by mincing the offal and stuffing it into the intestine. A visit to one of these restaurants left me feeling I had been to a culinary equivalent of a Soho strip club – not so much meeting the enemy as meating the enemy.

Sheila was an unusual but outstanding Tearfund worker, seconded to work with a Christian student initiative, particularly keen to find ways of encouraging indigenous Christian writing so that they could step out of the shadow of the USA. My first major discovery was that in Argentina full-time students also had a job. They had to, because they had to pay for their course. No grant, no loan – you spent the day working, the evening studying, the night sleeping at home. No campus, no halls of residence. Buenos Aires had half a million people doing this, many taking years to get their degree.

The second discovery was the seeds of revival. On one hand there was Pastor Anacondia, a Pentecostal preacher drawing huge crowds, with many claims of miraculous healing: I was particularly fascinated by the stories of visitors to his crusade meetings reporting that their teeth had been filled without them even requesting it! On the other hand there was the quiet but nonetheless remarkable story that at a little suburban church attached to a Bible college that I visited, they were regularly getting people coming on a Sunday straight off the street, just because they wanted to find out about Jesus. Neither of these miracles happen that often back here – but then the average English churchgoer would perhaps find both of them a little threatening.

Some of those I spoke to were convinced that the war, and recent history in general, was part of the explanation for revival. This was clearly a politicised society – there were political graffiti everywhere, even daubed across statues in the main squares; I had seen the 'mothers of the disappeared' in Plaza de Mayo with the pictures of the sons they feared they would never see again. The junta had hoped to unite the nation and bolster their crumbling popularity by a successful Malvinas campaign – their failure, and the nature of their failure, had left many disillusioned, searching elsewhere for hope and purpose.

There was also a background of rapid economic upheaval. One lady we were with went into a shop to buy some chewing gum. She came out and indicated she had spent on the gum the same amount she had spent on her flat ten years earlier. It gave a whole new meaning to inflation.

I remembered my most successful history lesson back in Thornton Heath, when to explain hyper-inflation in 1920s Germany I tore a five pound note in half. This gained the attention of the boys as little else, and enabled me to illustrate that money is only paper that people trust and believe is worth something – when that trust crumbles, so does its value. As the class left, one of the boys muttered to me, 'I don't believe you, those stories about inflation.' I felt it was a curious kind of success, to find a historical episode beyond the belief of a worldly-wise teenager.

He would have found the nation of Eva Peron an interesting mental challenge.

There was one final discovery to be made in Buenos Aires. I was taken to meet a man with three degrees; his most recent was a doctorate in theology. He was clearly an impressive intellectual, a citizen of a country with whom we were still at war. Did we talk theology? Did we talk politics? No. Or not exactly. Within minutes of meeting we were engaged in a friendly but animated debate about 'the hand of God'. And you will never guess: he was convinced Maradona's World Cup goal for Argentina against England had been perfectly fair, and I was equally convinced of the opposite. Our eyes are servants of our preconceptions. And few things matter to men as much as football.

We flew back Aerolineas Argentinas to Lisbon – an entire jumbo jet upholstered in soft black leather, no doubt relatively cheap on account of the number of hides stripped bare by the carnivores of the nation. We had criss-crossed a continent to meet Tearfund workers in all kinds of situations – by lagoons, in the world's great cities, at the tops of mountains and in the remotest plains. '*Jesus went through all the towns and villages,*' says the gospel-writer. He still does, through the commitment and obedience of his followers. And the task is still the same: healing, teaching and preaching; the whole gospel for the whole person – body, mind and spirit.

13

Smoke Gets in your Eyes

So now, you will visit my Temple
of debris, infection and blight.
Come, join me and my crumpled servants
for this is a true, holy site.

                                                        Stewart Henderson

This was to be my most ambitious communications project to
date – and Tearfund's. Its origin was not only in the effectiveness
of the earlier tours with Garth Hewitt, but also in the realisation
that while I still wanted to affirm the blessing of those who had
not seen but yet had believed, for most people it was the
experience of poverty that opened their eyes to its challenge.
Tearfund could not take thousands of people to see for themselves; but we might encourage thousands to come to a
performance that would enable them to see, and feel, by proxy. If
a few gifted artists travelled on their behalf, then their performance could convey the substance of reality. Art provokes emotion;
emotion can be a stimulus to involvement.

So it was an artistic if motley crew that set off for the
Philippines, the departure clouded by hearing news of the East
Midlands aircrash on the way to Heathrow. Garth was joined by
a good friend, Stewart Henderson, a Liverpool poet with a
mastery of language and a rapier wit. Stewart had also worked
with Geoffrey Stevenson, an extraordinarily talented mime artist.

Geoffrey and I had both worked with John Renfrew, who included height, stage lighting, design and general logistics among his many talents. John Muggleton, who had done a lot of work for Tearfund, was the film director. My task was to enable the gifts of music, words, movement and film to mesh together powerfully, creatively and effectively.

The plan was to make an initial visit to the Philippines, come home and give time to the creative process, then return to film with scripts established and material thought through. I felt it was important for the artists to work on and communicate a shared experience. Geoffrey, John and Stewart were very much new to the so-called Third World, and I hoped that they could help the event capture something of that initial impact.

The initial impact of Metro-Manila is of traffic, buildings and people. The traffic features the colourful jeepneys, jeeps stretched into minibuses, always crammed with people and always decorated lovingly and garishly by their owners. We were met and briefed by Jun Vencer, a lawyer and a pastor, then the director of Tearfund partner Philrads (Philippine Relief and Development Services) and later to become the first non-Western director of the World Evangelical Fellowship. Jun had been one of the key leaders of the large evangelical community in the Philippines as they had responded to the dramatic People Power revolution that had swept Cory Aquino into office.

We discovered that one of the locations chosen for our experience was his own home village, Nueva Sevilla on the island of Iloilo. It took a little island-hopping by plane to get there, including a stop at the airport where the snack bar menu included the enticing offer of 'dog on a stick'. The journey was well worth the effort. Nueva Sevilla was a small fishing community, almost idyllic in appearance. Blue skies, deep blue sea with a white sandy beach fringed by palm trees, colourful small fishing boats, picturesque thatched huts. People pay a fortune to holiday in a place like this, and Jun had been born there. He told us that his childhood had been very happy – he had not known he was poor until somebody told him.

We were met by Mike, the local pastor, and Susing his wife, who cooked a most delicious meal of local fish. We were introduced to Jun's mother, an elderly lady still there in the village which Jun had left in an almost Dick Whittington-like way. It was not the first time that I was struck at both the reality and the potential significance for the individual of the move from village to city, from poverty to relative wealth, from Third World to Western 'civilisation' – all in a short span. It used to happen in our own society; it still happens in developing countries. In Kenya I was told that half of the cabinet ministers had been born in mud huts in tribal villages. Jun certainly saw his own experience as an encouragement that poverty was not the final word – his autobiography is entitled *Poor Is No Excuse*.

We made the most of the enchantment of the setting. Wrapped wraith-like in our mosquito nets we slept on the floor of the hut, which was raised off the ground as a precaution against flooding and thus created an ideal home under the hut for the family pigs. They provided excellent cover for my notorious snoring, but not entirely successfully – I guessed that comments about working out which was worse, the pigs below or the pigs above, were probably aimed at me.

The next morning we were up at 4.00 a.m. to share in the fishing experience. It was magical. We set off in complete darkness, crossing the beach by torch-light and climbing into the boats. Then the small fleet put out to sea, lights twinkling. Slowly dawn appeared, and the fishermen set to work. The large and heavy nets were thrown overboard, then hauled in, the men working with a rhythmic display of muscular effort. The first haul was just four or five large fish, the second included a squid which spurted ink all over the floor of the boat and forced us to stand.

It was full daylight; the boats headed back to Nueva Sevilla, the fishermen cooking a breakfast of fish on little charcoal stoves in the boat – very Sea of Galilee. The whole morning was a wonderful experience. John Muggleton captured it on film absolutely brilliantly. Stewart wrote a sharply worded poem to accompany Geoffrey's simple mime of the physical effort of the fishermen.

Some time earlier I had seen Geoffrey perform a mime version of the whole creation story. I had thought it stunningly creative and enormously powerful. This idyllic seaside setting seemed to reflect all the beauty and potential of God's creation – so we filmed Geoffrey performing the piece standing on the sea-wall, silhouetted against the clear blue sky; and as he finished, the camera slowly zoomed back so that the reality of the Philippine fishing village came into focus. It provided a poignant and symbolic opening to the video we produced to complement the stage performance.

Of course the villagers were both fascinated and bemused by the whole exercise. We were fascinated too, as to how mime would be received. On the one hand it had no language and therefore needed no translation; on the other, it was an art-form unknown in the culture, therefore perhaps baffling. Geoffrey quickly won the hearts of the fishing community, performing an impromptu pastiche of the fishing process that communicated in the universal language of slapstick and was greeted with gales of laughter.

No sooner had he finished than the local sweet shop opened up. It was no more than the front of a thatched hut slightly converted to allow display of a limited range of goodies. What made it fascinating was the marketing technique employed to drum up trade. The owner wanted the children to come close enough to be tempted; what better than a television to draw a crowd?

How many televisions there were in Nueva Sevilla we were not sure, but the attraction was certainly there. It was only a battered fourteen-inch model, placed on a chair – but the children gathered. And they watched an aerobics class from Manila. It was the theatre of the absurd come to life, the clash of two worlds. The rich world, all gloss and Lycra, entertainment designed to counter the excesses of excess; the viewers, TB coughs and tatty T-shirts. The malnourished entertained by the pampered.

This moment symbolised the knife-edge of reality we uncovered in this apparent tropical paradise. Geoffrey's mime of creation ended with the fall; human beings made in God's image turning their backs on their Creator, and losing their place in paradise. The image was broken. I decided that our presentation and video would be called *Broken Image*. We would try and place the poverty and suffering in the context of God's creation. We would affirm the beauty and the potential for redemption, while exploring the reality beneath the surface.

In Nueva Sevilla the effects of the fall were painful, the resources to fight back apparently meagre. The local hospital had an X-ray room that had the name on the door, but nothing at all inside. The fishermen's physical labour left them exhausted, unable to work, by their early forties. That labour was becoming less and less productive: massive Japanese factory trawlers were operating a few miles away in international waters, dynamiting the sea, systematically extracting massive hauls and depleting the stocks that were the lifeblood of the village. The paradise was home to a battle for survival.

Children were the first-line casualties in this battle. As in so many Third World communities, many did not make it to their fifth birthday. The lives of the most vulnerable were crushed between the twin arms of the nutcracker of poverty. On one hand, poor sanitation and hygiene contributed to the prevalence of disease; the lack of accessible healthcare provision ensured a sad and full toll was exacted.

How could we help people understand this aspect of reality of life in a tropical paradise? We asked Mike and Susing if they knew of anyone in the village who might be willing to talk about their experience. Which was how I found myself interviewing Hidenia Tumangan on film, through an interpreter. Her story was simple yet deeply profound. It was made particularly poignant and sharp for me, because when I asked if it was OK to discover her age, I found out she was exactly the same age as my own wife – thirty-nine – and was married in the same year. Her life experience was so different, yet in the end the similarities – what we have in common as human beings – are most important.

'I have had eleven children, seven are still living. By 4.00 a.m. I am in the town asking a fish vendor for a supply of fish so I can sell it for a profit. My husband is already out fishing and his sister, who is not able to work because of her mental problems, she looks after the children. My dream is to earn enough money to put my children through high school, then they could get a job as a salesgirl in a big grocery store – they only take high school graduates. Last month my three-month-old baby caught measles. I could not afford to stay at home and at midday they came running to say the baby was very sick. I rushed home and back to the hospital, but the baby just died.'

As she told me this story her eyes began to fill with tears. The final indignity was that she had been given the wood to make the coffin and forced to borrow money to pay for a proper funeral. I had persuaded Hidenia to open up her raw wound for public inspection; I did not feel very good about it, although I recognised that her tears would undoubtedly bring home the reality of poverty in a way no statistic ever would. They would also nail the common Western assumption that somehow the frequency with which children died meant that mothers no longer cared. I asked whether she thought she would have more children. With a shrug and a weary sigh, she replied, 'My husband will want me to.'

I was just about to end the interview and allow us both to recover from the emotion of it, when I remembered that I had been told she was a Christian. I took a deep breath, and desperately hoped I was not being crassly insensitive: 'What does knowing Jesus mean to you?' I asked. Her face changed. A smile formed through the tears. 'I know that one day I will be with him in heaven,' she said.

I have reflected on this many times. In our society we rightly shy away from any impression that our faith and hope is simply 'pie in the sky when we die'. Yet in home group discussions I discover that in fact in our society of wealth and comfort there is very little anticipation of heaven. We actually struggle to imagine that it could be better than our life here, so we make slightly nervous jokes about our uncertainty as to whether we really want to spend eternity dressed in white and singing endless Graham Kendrick songs. Hidenia knew the hope that the Bible speaks of so powerfully: '*There will be no more death or mourning or crying or pain.*' She had not given up on this life; but she had no difficulty imagining that the life to come would be preferable.

In Surigao City, way down in the south of the country, we discovered that same hope expressed in a little bamboo hut built by Felipe and Tomasita by a rubbish dump over a tidal swamp. They had come in search of work, and squatted where they could. Even getting to the house was a major achievement. We had to walk along a series of planks, no more than a few inches thick, that were somewhat precariously balanced over the mud and water of the swamp. This was where I thought the film cameraman most earned his fee, because if I found it difficult to balance, at least I was not attempting the feat with a heavy 16mm film camera on my shoulder, my eye glued to its viewfinder.

We tried hard to capture on film the experience of walking to the house, and the impact it made when it came into view. The simple veranda was a mass of flowers, a splash of colour and care in a very bleak and unhealthy environment. Inside everything was neat and tidy; the few possessions were carefully arranged, and it was clear that Tomasita made every effort to keep the house clean. We filmed as best we could, given the small amount of room to manoeuvre. Then we discovered it really was a tidal swamp; the water was now almost up to the floor of the house, and most of the plank path was underwater. We had an enforced stay of a couple of hours taking in the reality of building a Christian home in the most unlikely and challenging circumstances.

Outside Surigao City Stewart could not keep himself out of the water. We had planned that each of the four video programmes intended to complement the stage performance would begin with an introduction from Stewart that would be slightly quirky and capture the attention of the viewer. We had been investigating just why the local church spent some of its time working together in the rice fields, and uncovered something of the economic stranglehold applied by the wealthy absentee landowner through exorbitant rents.

The result was that we were filming at the rice field, and Stewart had the bright idea that this could make a great setting for an intro. The quirkiness would stem from the fact that he would roll up his trouser legs, kneel in the paddy field mud and water, and give the impression he was standing by saying: 'One of the things not commonly known about me is that I am, in fact, thirteen foot six; at this moment there's more of me below the water than above.' The start was fine; but Stewart found it impossible to finish the few sentences accurately. Take followed take; the sun was beating down, and the pressure to get it right grew.

As the pressure grew, so did the difficulty of getting it right. Stewart was not helped by his growing conviction that unpleasant carnivorous monsters were hidden in the mud and water and eating at his legs. A mind wandering on to the full implications of its owner's willingness to sacrifice in the cause of art was not one focused on getting the words right. By Take 9 he had finally come to terms with this dilemma, and delivered an intro that we all agreed, merciful beings that we were, would be acceptable.

In Manila I found myself hauled into the slightly surreal world of the filming process. Garth had written a song about injustice, inspired by the astonishing collection of shoes belonging to Imelda Marcos that had been uncovered in the Presidential Palace after the revolution. One particular pair had caught his eye during a brief visit – disco-dancing shoes that had built-in flashing lights. So the song began 'Imelda Marcos' disco-dancing shoes dance on the poor', and Stewart wanted to introduce the song by pretending to discover the shoes on a rubbish dump. Obvious.

Curiously, we did not think the authorities would let us borrow the shoes for this purpose, so I was despatched to try and discover something similar. Off I went to the local shopping mall, and into the shoe section. This was when I realised that I had a choice. I could either attempt to explain what I was looking for in English to an assistant who might or might not speak English, and who might or might not be an ardent Marcos supporter; or I could look around the shelves of ladies' shoes, trying not to look embarrassed.

I opted for this second approach, but was not allowed to pursue it for long. A helpful shop assistant came over. 'Can I help you?' she enquired. I decided I had to brazen it out. 'I'm looking for the brightest, most outrageous shoes you have in stock.' Her face did not flicker. 'What size would you require, sir?' This natural but completely unexpected question floored me, and I blurted out, 'It doesn't matter, any size will do.' This particular lady confirmed all the stereotype inscrutability of the oriental, expressing no surprise at all at this foreign man who wanted to buy a pair of ladies' shoes, size immaterial. She returned with a pair of very high heeled shoes covered in multi-coloured sequins. Ideal. I'm not sure what the auditors made of my expense claim when I returned home.

* * *

It was almost an afterthought to visit Smoky Mountain. It had become a kind of tourist landmark in Manila, much to the disgust of most of its citizens. Why did visitors want to go and see the city's rubbish dump? John Muggleton had already seen it; he was keen that the rest of us should see it for ourselves. Within minutes of our arrival we knew it was the place that would offer a powerful symbol and setting for *Broken Image*.

The rubbish dump had started with refuse simply being tipped into the sea. The mound had grown; it was now a few hundred feet high, and its insides were on fire. It was called Smoky Mountain because it was a mountain that smoked. Smoke wisped up in some places; in others, flames and thick, acrid smoke billowed into the sky. At one point I was standing, trying to describe the scene into a cassette recorder, when flames suddenly burst through the ground just a few feet away.

Smoky Mountain was home to about four thousand families. They had built houses from the rubbish, from wooden pallets, plywood sheets, packing cases and polythene. The foot of the mountain was surrounded by these homes; they extended up either side of the path to the top. Their inhabitants made their living by scavenging through the rubbish, sifting through the rotting vegetables for anything of value. It was recycling, at a high level of personal risk and involvement. Bright yellow dustbin lorries, an aid gift from the people of Japan, made their way up to the top of the mountain at regular intervals, one every few minutes. At the top their load was tipped out, and the scavengers immediately closed in, each hoping that they would make the lucky strike.

When we first arrived, we just stared. It was an awesome sight. Bulldozers rolled backwards and forwards across the top of the hill; the scavengers worked away steadily and purposefully. I gradually noticed that some were children, as young as six or seven; some were old. There were men and women, all dressed in rags, some with cloth masks tied round their nose and mouth as a rudimentary air filter. There was even a man with one leg, balanced on his crutches, picking through the garbage with his home-made sorting and collecting implement.

The key moment came when we suddenly realised that there was order among the chaos. All had baskets over their shoulders, many specialised in collecting drink cans. When their baskets were full, they would leave them on a mat, which seemed to identify them as theirs. They would then set off back across the mountain with an empty basket, leaving the full one unattended. It suddenly struck me that this involved a great deal of trust. In a church hall jumble sale you would not take this risk. A lady once left her new umbrella unattended at my church's missionary garden party and within a few minutes it had been sold for 50p. Here were these people, living and working in desperate conditions, struggling for survival, and yet prepared to effectively trust their wealth to others.

This seething, festering heap of garbage seemed to offer a microcosm of the Third World experience. The smoke almost obscured the view. It was hard to imagine a more unpleasant, unhealthy environment. It was difficult to believe that poverty could make anyone more desperate than to live and work literally on the refuse of the rich. And yet there was something positive. Human resilience was making recycling the basis of a way of life. Something good was being created and retrieved from the dirt and filth. There was laughter and productivity. The image might be broken but it was not destroyed. A little boy had picked up an old record and was throwing it like a frisbee. It landed at my feet, and I stooped to read the label: Frank Sinatra, 'Don't Throw Your Dreams Away'.

Curiously, a large cross had been erected on the top of Smoky Mountain, a powerfully symbolic reminder of one who died on a rubbish dump outside a city wall so that broken and worthless human lives could be recycled and renewed by their maker. It gave the ultimate perspective to the view. As we made our way down off the mountain, we saw a rickety, almost caricature version of a church, complete with an attempt at a spire. It was wonderfully named 'The Co-workers' Baptist Church' and we were introduced to its pastor, Antonio Senora.

He had stowed away on a boat to get to Manila so he could seek his fortune. He had become a Christian and come to Smoky Mountain seventeen years earlier because he was convinced that God had called him to bring good news to the poor. He had not only established the church, but had tried to obtain land rights for the squatters on the dump. The cost had been heavy – the previous year his youngest daughter had died of pneumonia. But he was still convinced that he must stay until God called him to go elsewhere.

One of his congregation lived in the first house as the road entered the dump. Like the others, it was built from bits of wood and other odds and ends. Beltran Banzuelo was in his twenties. He worked the night shift – as the numbers grew there had been fighting, and a shift system of sorts had been introduced – climbing the mountain just before sunset to spend the night sifting the rubbish for tin cans. He had not always been a scavenger; his government clerical job had disappeared with the fall of Marcos.

Now we discovered that his scavenging supported an extended family of seven, which included his sister Helen. Even more remarkably, Beltran earned enough to pay for Helen to go through teacher training college. We watched her set out for college, her best (and only) dress immaculate, her books under her arm. And we discovered that Beltran had a dream: he too wanted to train, to go to Bible college and become a pastor.

We told Beltran's story in *Broken Image*. Someone who had just begun Bible college here offered to pay for Beltran to be able to complete high school and go on to train as a pastor. It was a considerable outlay, because the support costs for seven people had to be covered. But I was able to make the arrangements, and the first result was a letter, half in English and half in Tagalog, his own language, that expressed his thanks. It was strange to think of a letter arriving from that first house on a smoking rubbish dump.

When I got home, I decided that if Beltran could live, and more, by recycling, then the least I could do was to follow his example and recycle as much of our household rubbish as possible – after all, it was a little easier for me than it was for him. Of course, it was easy for me to make the decision – something my wife reminds me of every time she cuts her hand washing out a baked beans tin.

Three years later I had the opportunity to return. Antonio and Beltran were still there, Beltran had started college. There were now four churches on Smoky Mountain; hundreds of the scavengers had come to know Christ. The cross on the top had collapsed as the mountain's insides burned themselves hollow and caved in as more rubbish piled on; but the life made possible by the cross was breaking out. When Smoky Mountain was eventually razed by government decree, the squatters christened their new tenement blocks Paradise Mountain.

We saw beauty in the ashes
We saw treasure in the dust
We saw joy come out of mourning
We saw diamonds in the rough.
And though the image may look broken
We saw Jesus shining through
And on each forgotten feature
He was writing 'I love you.'

This was Garth's closing song of *Broken Image*. Twenty-two thousand people shared the experience. Thousands more have studied the video material. Some wrote and told me their lives had been changed.

14

Up the Patuca without a Paddle

This is your land, it's the way it was planned
Sky to the sea, something to see
This is your land, laid out in your hand

You don't know what you've got till the whole thing's gone
The days are dark and the road is long
And when you walk away, the hope is gone
Tell me what is right, and what is wrong

Wherever I go, way down here I know
This is your land

Simple Minds

This was remote. Heathrow to Miami one day; Miami to La Ceiba, Honduras, via Belize the next; up at 5.00 a.m. the third day to catch the small plane, helpfully equipped with three pilots. Its first attempt at landing was aborted, because there were horses eating the grass airstrip. The second attempt was successful, and we transferred to dugout canoe to travel up the Rio Tinto. Once again I was on the Mosquito Coast of Honduras, due to play a starring role in the Tearfund epic *Terry and the Chocolate Factory*.

That would explain why the video director was called Terry, who was also the sound recordist; oddly, both the cameraman and the photographer were called Mike, surely a more appropriate

133

name for the sound recordist. Photographer Mike was Mike Webb – a long-standing colleague, *Tear Times* editor, occasional wearer of astounding pony-tail and bermuda shorts, a genuinely intrepid world traveller and a kind of renaissance man for the new millennium.

The canoe had an outboard motor, and we made steady progress up the river. It was almost still, incredibly peaceful; a private boat trip into the depths of the tropical rainforest. Occasionally we disturbed herons on the bank; they flapped lazily into the sky as we passed. Sometimes a canoe went past in the opposite direction, perhaps with a family on board, or with someone clearly on their way to or from market, their canoe loaded with fruit, or sacks of food. But for most of the time there was just us, the river and the forest.

As we came round a bend in the river a very English pastoral scene came into view. Cattle were grazing by the riverbank; apart from the heat, we could have been punting on the Cam. That was when I noticed that the Indian pastor who was travelling with us had tears in his eyes. What was there about this peaceful idyll that could possibly have upset him? The answer was simple: the cattle were grazing where six weeks earlier there had been forest. The chainsaws had left their mark. Now the land and the riverbank would be ruined, effluent and soil would get into the river, the fish would be affected, and the whole livelihood of the pastor's flock would be at risk. Hours and hours of travel, but it took only minutes to get to the heart of the problem.

This one scene captured the essence of a major global environmental catastrophe; the threatened rainforest has become almost a Western media cliché, but the tears in the eyes of an Indian pastor reminded me not only of its devastating reality, but that it is a reality that ultimately affects people. The Miskito Indians have lived in this forest for centuries. They know how to live from it and with it; it is their major resource, to be used, respected and protected. Part of the area is an almost unique

Mother Teresa examines the Tearfund calender presented by
Stephen Rand (centre) and Garth Hewitt, Calcutta 1982
(*photo: Tony Neeves*)

An unexpected shower – the EFICOR drilling-rig breaks
through, India 1982 (*photo: Tony Neeves*)

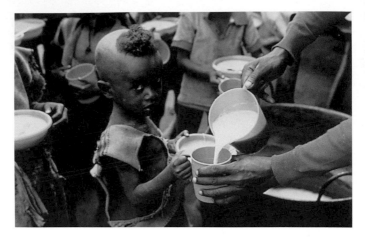

Tearfund and SIM relief in the Ethiopian famine, 1984
(photo: Tony Neeves)

Chuclalas village, Peru: Marie-Christine Lux in action,
shortly before guinea pig is served, 1987
(photo: Stephen Rand)

Smoky Mountain, Manila, Philippines, 1989
(photo: Greenleaf)

Flight over the rainforest, Honduras, 1990
(photo: Mike Webb)

Rene Drabo faces the interview ordeal, Burkina Faso, 1991
(photo: Mike Webb)

The breathtaking Sao Paulo skyline, 1991
(photo: Jim Loring)

The cross above the Lima shanties, 1991
(photo: Jim Loring)

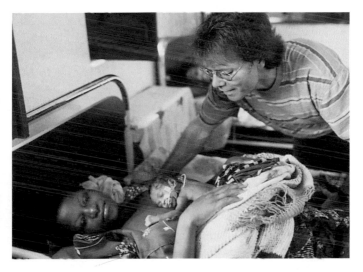

Sir Cliff Richard meets Sarah Maseraka and baby Masika,
Kagando Hospital, Uganda, 1992 *(photo: Jim Loring)*

One of the twenty-eight weddings at Armonia,
Mexico City, 1994 *(photo: Richard Hanson)*

Destruction in the streets of Kabul, Afghanistan, 1996
(photo: Zeba Media)

Vijayan and Premila
Pavamani, India

Florence Yeboah, Ghana

Andy Meakins, Addis
Ababa, Ethiopia

Pilar and Saúl Cruz,
Mexico City

Joseph Knight points out home, Liberia, across the river.
Guinea, 1997 *(photo: Richard Hanson)*

Terry Gibson and Stephen Rand interview David and
Emmanuel from SECADOS, Guinea, 1997
(photo: Richard Hanson)

expanse of tropical pine forest; it is included in a United Nations designated Biosphere Reserve, intended for special protection because of its ecological value. Tearfund's partner MOPAWI is a Christian organisation founded to assist the Indian people of Mosquitia, and has realised that to do so it must help them to protect their environment.

The next morning we rapidly discovered this was a real battle. We went to interview Reynaldo Alvarez, Inspector of Resources for the Biosphere Reserve. He had a simple enough philosophy: 'The Biosphere is like a box of resources,' he said, 'it should not be emptied out but kept for the good of the nation. That is what God wants us to do.' So that is why he had taken on some relatives of the Honduran President who had slaughtered 5,000 crocodiles, each one killed for a small area of skin from its stomach which made the best shoes and handbags. He thought that explained the death threat he had received. Almost unbelievably to me, he really had received an envelope containing a bullet with his name on it. I asked him how seriously he took it. 'It costs about $50 to hire a gunman around here,' he chillingly replied.

Reynaldo was clear about the issues and the causes. He was convinced that Mosquitia's remoteness and isolation were its only hope of survival. He knew that plans were being made to extend the road from the capital city, Tegucigalpa, deep into the reserve. It would be a road too far for the forest and its people. He rejected the suggestion that it was the desperation of the poor Latino farmers in the rest of Honduras that created the pressure; he had no doubt: it was the greed of wealthy cattle ranchers and loggers that promoted the road as a means to simplify their business and maximise their profits.

Once the road was there, it would be a bridgehead for the poor farmers to use to pour on to the land, to slash and burn to prepare for their crops, and see the land ruined and unproductive within two or three years. Reynaldo was pessimistic. 'When the road comes it will be all over,' he said, 'and nothing can stop the road.' His faith in God did not run to expecting this particular miracle. I felt that all I could offer was that I would encourage people to pray for him.

At that moment we heard a gunshot. It was not very far away. Reynaldo seemed unconcerned, so we too tried to look nonchalant. When we emerged from his house, we discovered that there had indeed been a victim. There was a scene of fearful carnage just yards away. Blood was flowing down the street, there seemed to be innards everywhere. A man was wielding a fearful-looking axe to dismember the body. A crowd had gathered. The butcher's stall was about to open, and very fresh beef was available.

We carried on to interview the pastor who had travelled with us the day before. The Miskito Indians are mainly Moravians, converted as a result of a nineteenth century missionary effort. He remembered with great affection the English missionary who had introduced him to Jesus, who had stayed with the people so long that eventually he had to be carried to the boat to take him home. He also remembered how upset he had been by his experience the day before. He too was deeply pessimistic about the future.

The MAF flight into the interior did nothing to dispel the gloom. High above the forest we could see plumes of smoke on the horizon, evidence of the continuing destruction. We landed at the airstrip at Wampusirpe, then moved on by boat to Santa Isabel. It was time for my big moment, my starring role.

Terry Gibson, our video director on this trip, has over the years worked with me on a whole variety of projects. One of his specialities has been videos for primary age children, using animation to tell stories and help develop understanding of mission and Third World realities. One problem has always been cost; the children are used to seeing expensive and sophisticated television cartoons. Terry, along with Taffy Davies, his cartoonist accomplice, has produced a number of videos, high on creativity and low on cost, making the most of the technology currently available.

These productions starred Terry Tearaway, the cartoon character who featured in a regular magazine for children, and who reported to them on what was happening around the world. So while we were making the video for Tearfund's harvest focus later that year, we were also taking the opportunity to allow Terry Tearaway to make a video. The technique Terry was using (Terry Gibson, pay attention) for this one was to shoot live action from about the eye-line of a ten-year-old, and also some scenes into which Terry (Tearaway – come on, it's not that difficult) would be inserted by overlay back in the studio.

My job was to be Terry. I had to pretend to be the height of a ten-year old so that others would appear to be reacting sensibly to Terry Tearaway on the finished product. Have you got the picture? I had to look stupid in Honduras, and then I would be overlaid and disappear in the studio. Some starring role. It certainly baffled the locals.

The chocolate theme was derived from a particular project. MOPAWI was assisting the Indians to grow and market cocoa. Cocoa was apparently an excellent crop for the rainforest: it could grow in the shade of the huge trees, and therefore be cultivated without damaging the forest. The crop was being made into cooking chocolate by a relatively simple process, and then taken out of the region by boat and sold in the capital. The Indians earned some badly needed cash, and the forest was spared.

The plan was that Hernaldo would show Terry how the cooking chocolate was made. He would start with the trees in the forest, he would see how the pods were split open, and the fleshy pith removed. He would see the beans being minced and then being poured into the mould. Then the highlight moment, when Hernaldo presented him with a finished block of cooking chocolate. That was when Terry actually appeared, and therefore when I appeared.

The final act took place on the veranda of Hernaldo's house, and so it was that, watched by a curious group of children and by a puzzled Hernaldo, I tried to reduce my height by about two feet and walk forward at the same time to receive the chocolate. The result was an Oscar-winning, knee-bending shuffle, and I made a mental note never to work with animals and children. Fortunately the giggles from the bystanders could be removed from the soundtrack, and in the finished product a happy Terry stepped smoothly forward to receive his chocolate. *Terry and the Chocolate Factory* won no awards, other than the plaudits of grateful parents and teachers who were delighted that there was something positive, informative and wholesome that really did engage the attention of children.

That evening we ate a simple meal, then sat on the bluff gazing down at the Rio Patuca in the moonlight, while fireflies played in the trees, and the Indians sang softly around the fire. A child of the sixties would have called it mellow, the more biblically reflective might have sensed something of the *shalom* of the Creator. It was memorable.

The alarm went off at 4.00 a.m., and by 5.00 we were in the dugout heading up the Patuca. The moon was still bright on the water, then gradually the dawn light filtered through the mist rising from the river, from where it seemed to be caught and held for nourishment in the canopy of the forest. By 11.00 a.m. we had reached our destination, Krausirpe, an Indian village deep in the forest. It was hard to imagine a more remote setting. There was a deep sense of privilege that we had been allowed to come so far and see this hidden treasure of the creation.

Suddenly, late afternoon, a different reality arrived. They seemed to come from nowhere, but when they arrived, they arrived. Hundreds of Americans. I think it was actually only about fifteen, but it certainly seemed like more. Perhaps it was military training: I mean, they were organised and they organised. 'Mellow' was a word they would have chewed up and spat out. It was awesome. They were very definitely on a mission from God. There was a dental clinic to set up, a clothes handout to be seen to. They gave two weeks of their annual vacation to this, and they were not going to waste time.

They hardly seemed to notice us. They were focused; the presence of a British video crew in the depths of the Honduran jungle caused no obvious surprise or interest. We all camped down for the night in the schoolroom of the village, and slept fitfully. The next morning one of them spoke to me. I discovered they were from Wyoming.

We began the journey back. An hour or so down the river there was a ferocious shower, rain sheeting down as if a cosmic bucket had been poured over the Biosphere to water the forest. There was an umbrella in the boat, so I attempted to keep myself dry by raising it, only to discover that the wind and the movement of the canoe meant that it had to be held out almost in front of me like a shield. After a few minutes it was over, and the sun reappeared and began to create a natural sauna. I left the umbrella up in front of me to dry out, and managed to achieve a new sleeping posture, my chin cradled on the rim of the extended nylon.

I have built a solid reputation at Tearfund for my ability to fall asleep in almost any location and any posture. In fact, there is even a growing series of photographs: Stephen Rand sleeps – on church steps in Addis Ababa, on a train in Bangladesh, in a minibus in West Africa. But I feel that the open umbrella in the dugout canoe was perhaps my finest hour.

After the canoe, we walked a mile or so to reach the nearest airstrip, where we waited for the tiny MAF plane to come and pick us up. It was a long wait, so Terry, Mike Webb and I decided that this was the moment to video a scene for *Carry On Tearfund*.

On our walk from the village we had been accompanied by a crowd of children, who seemed very anxious to help by carrying something for us. One of the men with us had an old rifle slung over his shoulder, so I asked if I could borrow it.

The camera was set up. First I appeared, rifle nonchalantly in place, staring confidently towards the uncharted regions that lay ahead. I was followed by a file of twenty bearers, starting with the tallest, carefully graded down to the youngest and smallest, who were probably no more than five or so. Every one was carrying something on their head: David Livingstone meets Indiana Jones. Curiously, we have never found a use for this epic sequence.

The plane came, and we quickly turned from the slapstick to the serious as the pilot flew us over the Biosphere Reserve. The hills rolled on to the horizon, each covered with a green mantle of trees. It was if a lumpy olive-green carpet had been laid for as far as the eye could see. Some of the hills were extraordinary shapes; others appeared as anchorages for the clouds that seemed to be born in the forest and then lazily released into the atmosphere. Mike Webb, our stills photographer, was ecstatic. Whereas the large video camera was difficult to manoeuvre and was forced to shoot through the perspex, Mike could point his trusty Nikon through the small opening possible in the tiny plane.

The pilot was most obliging, turning and twisting round a sugarloaf-shaped hill so that Mike could find the best angle for a stunning photograph. He found it. We turned the tiny slide into a giant poster with the text 'The earth is the Lord's' and it was seen in churches all over Britain. Every time I see it I remember not only the view, but also the stomach-churning flight that made it possible. I also recall that immediately after it, there was the untold luxury of a shower, a toilet, an electric fan and a bed.

The final stage of the visit was to Puerto Lempira. It had been the home of the rat that I had feared would get me between the light switch and the bed. It was now not only a place with a clean hotel, but also, more importantly, home to some Tearfund workers, partly as a result of Jennifer Loughlin's conversations on that previous visit.

Andrew Leake had been accompanying us on our flights and canoe visits. He had even been awarded the honour of a video interview by Terry Tearaway! His work was focused on helping the Indians protect the forest and themselves, by obtaining legal rights to the land, and by persuading the government to create a larger reserve alongside the Biosphere Reserve. There were parallels to the situation in the Chaco, where Andrew had grown up with his missionary parents. His wife Maria was from Argentina, and her job was to maximise the opportunities for publicising the situation in Mosquitia as a means of protecting the Indians. The Latino population of Honduras lived in the west of the country; many hardly knew the Indians and their forest home existed.

Rick James was concentrating on the business enterprise aspect of MOPAWI's work. MOPAWI was almost completely responsible for the economic infrastructure that existed for the Indians inland, running a chain of tiny shops, buying beans and cocoa from the Indians, and marketing it on their behalf. Cathy, Rick's wife, and Paul Stephenson were teachers. Tearfund by policy did not normally supply teachers, but here the need was specialist and acute: there was no teaching available to the Indians in their own languages, and the government curriculum was inevitably based on the needs of the populous Spanish-speaking end of the country.

They were all based in Puerto Lempira, the biggest town in Mosquitia, situated on the shores of the lagoon. The biggest, but not that big. Electricity came on at six and went off at nine thirty, until the municipal generator ran out of diesel. Remaining supplies were conserved for Saturday nights only, until the next boat of supplies arrived. We became regulars at the three cafés that were at all safe for us to use: eggs and beans at Bambu's for breakfast, enchiladas at Delmy's for dinner, and sometimes – a special treat – steak and chips at Yampu's. This was not by choice, but actually the full extent of the menu at each establishment. One night the desert of dessert became too much, and in a riot of risk and extravagance, and against all the official Tearfund advice to travellers, we ordered ice cream – rum and raisin. Ominously the raisins were all at the bottom of the helpings, suggesting that it had melted and been refrozen. We didn't care. This was the year of living dangerously.

The lagoon offered us one more opportunity to fill out the story of Mosquitia. There was a strong wind blowing as we crossed it, the boat bouncing around like a cork. After about an hour we reached the thin strip of land that separated the lagoon from the open sea. Cathy and Paul took us to see the schools. To our surprise the first was called 'Inglaterra'. The reason was even more surprising. Apparently it fell out with the other school around the time of the Falklands War; when we arrived there we discovered it was named 'Argentina'.

The children demonstrated that they were expert at getting the nuts off the cashew tree; they were also pretty good at drawing, as, unusually for a Third World school, there were crayon pictures up on the walls. They featured boats and divers; Cathy explained they had put diving on their curriculum. Diving was a great way for the young men to earn a living. The boat-owners came and took them on, and they could make a reasonable living diving for lobster for American restaurant tables.

The problem was a complete lack of training and safety instruction. Spurred on by the demands of the captains, they would dive repeatedly and deeply, and many had terrifying attacks of the bends. They had no clue what was happening to them, or what had caused it; some of the young men blamed the spirits of the deep. We met one of the victims, Arquimedes Lopez: at just nineteen completely paralysed, lying face-down and motionless on the bed. Exploited, unprotected, and vulnerable in his ignorance; now destroyed.

Destruction in paradise is a recurring Third World theme. 'Call some place paradise, kiss it goodbye,' was The Eagles summary in a bitter song which includes a hefty side-swipe at the impact of the missionary. The visit to the Honduran rainforest convinced me that New Age concern for the environment misses the essential Christian understanding that human beings have a special place in the global life-support system. More than just another animal, they alone can and must take decisions that demonstrate concern and care for the planet; and those decisions must take into account the poorest and most vulnerable human beings who are the first victims of environmental disaster.

But Christians too have to come to terms with environmental concern. When Tearfund joined forces with Youth for Christ and Spring Harvest for the *Whose Earth?* youth focus around the time of the Rio Summit in 1992, it was fascinating to discover how few adult Christians really were prepared to respond positively to the environmental agenda. Many seemed convinced that it was a New Age topic; an argument effectively dealt with by the adoption of the term 'creation care', which at least encapsulates something of the basic but essential teaching that God made our environment, he is responsible for sustaining it, and he has entrusted its care to human beings.

When I have spoken on this topic in churches, the reaction of young people is perhaps not surprising; they are delighted to discover that the church has something to say on this subject. They have heard about it at school; every survey of youth concerns lists the environment as their number one issue, yet the church usually offers them no more than a deafening silence or a hostile reaction. It is more than sad; it is unbiblical and catastrophic in its effect.

The encouraging thing about Honduras is that Christians

remain at the forefront of the battle for the Indian people and their environment. Tearfund helped by encouraging people to back an international campaign and fax or e-mail the Honduran President when he proposed to offer a concession to a logging company to extract timber from Mosquitia; the campaign was successful.

I have discovered that raising a banner for creation-care may involve inconvenience, insult, even taking risks. That was certainly my experience the day we left Puerto Lempira. We were woken at 4.00 a.m. by a colossal explosion; it sounded as if a bomb had gone off outside our hotel window. There were a few seconds' silence in the aftermath, as if the sound-waves from the blast had blown all other sounds clear away. But no such luck. Because then the band started to play. It was loud, it was off-key, it was awful, it was 4.01 in the morning. I don't know what they were celebrating, but it seemed like a good moment to leave.

Up at the airstrip the pilot of our little plane looked at us, then at our luggage, then at us. Then he looked again. Then the scales were produced. The luggage was weighed, and then we were weighed. I was affronted. They said I was sixteen stone. The weight was called out to everyone. I protested: the scales were obviously faulty, in fact they were in error, heretical. It was no good. Someone, and some of the luggage would have to stay. I might have been the heaviest, but I was still in charge. So someone else was volunteered, but I was still seething about the lying scales when we arrived in Tegucigalpa.

It was great to have some reading matter available to take my mind off the insult. On the plane itself it was fascinating to find an MAF accident report stuffed down the side of the seat. It helpfully explained how a plane had successfully crash-landed on to the rainforest canopy, gently settling itself on to the web of branches more than hundred feet from the forest floor. The only fatality was someone who got out of the plane and fell through the branches. No sooner had this eye-opener been digested than I was reading the tourist magazine offered to all new arrivals at Tegucigalpa. This had a feature article explaining why it was impossible to build a safe international airport for the capital city because of its position in the mountains. Meanwhile, Honduran television was showing a plane that had overshot a local runway being towed back out of the sea. Perhaps you really are closer to God when you fly.

15

Careless Whisper

On your journey 'cross the wilderness
From the desert to the well
You have strayed upon the motorway to Hell.

Chris Rea

I was sweating in the airport queue. Had I blown it? Was I going to be refused entry to a country for the first time in my travelling career? The whole trip had already got off to a bad start. We had found it impossible to persuade the Ghanaian embassy to give us our visas in time to catch the flight that had been booked, and we had left Gatwick at 1.00 a.m., more than two days late. Now it was 6.00 a.m. local time, but I was awake enough to hear the person two ahead of me in the queue being asked for their vaccination certificate. I had carried this with me on every trip for the past ten years, and I had never been asked for it. I looked in the front of my Filofax: that was where I kept it. It was not there.

Then I remembered: I had taken it out when I had done my latest impression of a pin-cushion at the doctor's, and it was almost certainly in my jacket pocket. The problem was, I don't travel with a jacket. Now the person in front of me was being asked for his certificate. I could not believe it. Two days late, and I was going to be put back on the plane and sent whence I came, all for a bit of paper. Panic, sweat and prayer poured out of me. It was my turn. I stepped forward, hoping desperately that the health officer would assume sweat was a sign of heat rather than guilt. He looked me up and down, and waved me through, saying nothing. As I picked up my case and moved on, I heard him ask the next person for their certificate.

We were met outside by Florence Yeboah, the director of GHACOE Women's Ministry, whose projects were the focus of our visit to Ghana. Florence is one of the most dynamic and formidable leaders I have ever met. She had been trained at London Bible College, taken on an evangelism role in the most dangerous streets of Harlem, New York, and now she was back in her own country. Her organisation had been formed when a group of women attending a conference – the GHAna Conference On Evangelism – had decided they were tired of listening to men talking, and determined to do something with and for and through the women of Ghana.

Florence was quick to emphasise the role and significance of women in Africa. They do the bulk of the agricultural labour and they raise the children – 'Educate a man, and you educate an individual; educate a woman and you educate the nation,' said Florence with a big smile and great conviction, quoting a Ghanaian philosopher. So they had set about the task of educating women: about health and childcare, about nutrition and food preparation, about agriculture and dressmaking, about Jesus. Florence was overseeing all this, regularly preaching at evangelistic healing and deliverance meetings in the evenings, encouraging women to grow cassava and give their children fruit drinks during the day.

Her energy, her gifts, her commitment and the range of her concerns were extraordinary. There are two of her prayers I particularly recall: at a Tearfund Conference at Swanwick, Derbyshire, when she rebuked the devil and his works in ringing tones of authority – afterwards she commented, 'The devil always seems so much more polite in England than he is in Africa'; the next day, in our home, she prayed for Katharine, then aged fourteen, and included a powerful prayer for the man that she would marry. We were glad of her confidence in praying well in advance of the event! Florence is a prime example of both the accuracy and the inaccuracy of the oft-quoted adage: 'God's method is God's man.' The hideous sexism is both biblically and experientially false, the significance of the inspirational visionary in bringing about positive change undeniable.

Within minutes of meeting Florence we had not only begun to appreciate her many qualities; we had also received a hint of the travelling that was to come. Accra was jammed with traffic moving very slowly, not least because of the attempts to avoid the enormous potholes in the road surface. A trip of one mile each way to visit the post office so that I could phone home and try to retrieve my vaccination certificate took two hours – an hour on the roads, an hour queuing up to use the phone. Welcome to West Africa.

Welcome to West Africa indeed! The next two days were an extraordinary mix of enthusiastic welcomes and frustrating bureaucracy. After the team had been installed in the Theresita Royal Hotel, and much to their amusement Florence had insisted that as leader I should have the Royal Suite (not as grand as it sounds), we were taken to her headquarters. We were greeted by a group of women singing a chorus with great enthusiasm; they were all wearing GHACOE T-shirts, some with the slogan 'Grace in abundance' in bold lettering across their chests. Again I was carefully identified as the leader, and given a bunch of flowers by a very shy and very beautiful girl. This was obviously the trip that was to be my recompense for that earlier arduous experience of regularly being designated 'staff'.

It got even better the next day. We had seen some of the project activities in the Accra headquarters; now we were at the farm out in the country, watching the women planting cassava. This is a surprisingly simple process, involving taking an old stalk, chopping off a few inches and burying one end in the ground. The women were doing this at a tremendous rate; the tip of the machete would be used to make a small hole, the end of the stalk would be pushed into it, then *thwack*, the machete would slice off the end. It took a few seconds, and the whole field was planted in minutes.

Then Florence explained it was time for me to meet the local village chief. But this was not a quick greeting and a handshake; this was to be a full ceremonial *durbar*. I thought I had perhaps heard this word before. Wasn't it the way the Queen was greeted when she went to India? Anyway, we were taken to a large flat area in the middle of the village. On one side there was a canopy over a number of chairs, where we were taken to sit. On the other side, about twenty metres away, was another row of seats. As we watched a file of men came and sat down. This was the chief and his elders.

There was a kind of official organiser who clutched his notes and shouted instructions, rushing backwards and forwards to oversee the ceremony. He indicated the opening routine. One by one we all were taken across the square to shake hands with the chief and his elders, then we returned to our seats. Then a lady was asked to pray. It was almost as if a dam had burst. She prayed, she led everyone into song, prayed some more, encouraged more singing; it was enthusiastic, vibrant and powerful, and it went on for twenty minutes.

This prepared the ground for the chief to speak. He made a solemn speech which included a formal request for water and electricity for his village. As the visiting chief I had to respond. I did my best to match him in solemnity, which was not easy, for I sensed that my travelling companions were finding the idea of my chief-like, royal treatment just a little amusing. I hoped that they would learn from the respect I was being shown. What finished them off was that the speeches were followed by the exchanging of gifts. I was led out into the middle of the square and with more due solemnity presented with a sheep, a bowl of pineapples and a crate of Pepsi-Cola.

I don't think the crew's sniggering was either noticed or helpful; I kept my face straight and out of the corner of my mouth asked Florence her assessment of the etiquette of the situation. She immediately whispered some brilliant advice, and I turned back to the chief. I thanked him for the honour that had been done to me and my team, and explained that I felt the best way of accepting his gift would be to ask the women on the GHACOE farm to look after the sheep on my behalf. By now the crew had descended into a fantasy built around the possibility that the sheep would have many lambs that would all be called Rand in my honour. It was time to go.

Florence took us on to another project, this time a small cassava processing plant. It was an interesting series of activities, turning the root into flour in a way that removed its poison and made it an income-generating project. Here I began a parallel career to that of great white chief. Videoing the process was made quite difficult by the children crowding around, so I had the bright idea that I might be able to provide some distracting entertainment. What could I do that would be more interesting than a large video camera? I went out of the building to the tiny court-yard and found myself, against my better judgment, racing crowds of children up and down. They were shrieking with laughter. When, exhausted, I decided that perhaps dispensing sweets would give the crew a little more breathing space, I opened two or three packets of Fizzers and was nearly trampled to death in the rush.

I should perhaps introduce the team. I was working with a new video company, who had the advantage of being based in Birmingham, and had done an excellent job in making a youth video for me featuring the astonishing communication talents of American preacher and sociologist Tony Campolo. Sally Murcutt was the co-owner of CVG, along with her husband Aden. Sally has become a good friend; she is quick-witted, creative and excellent company, with an interesting way of sporting a startling new hair colour for each overseas visit. Sally was accompanied by Helen Jowett, who was directing the video; it was fascinating travelling with two women on the team – they had brought a silver flight case that looked as if it contained high-powered technical equipment, but from which little domestic comforts like hot chocolate and biscuits, even Earl Grey tea, would appear at just the right moment.

Trevor Burgess was the experienced professional cameraman – experienced, but then not widely travelled. He took a kind of laid-back but sharp-eyed interest in all that was going on. Then there was Derrick Thomson, the Scottish sound recordist with a limitless range of jokes, some of which were funny; he also had an uncanny skill of mimicry, which first emerged on the aircraft when he did such a good impression of the intercom that he was able to persuade several passengers to fasten their seatbelts. Add in to this pressure cooker full of creative talent the inimitable Mike Webb, then you can understand the awesome responsibilities that being the official chief involved.

One of them was to look after the money. This was a major exercise in itself. There were 600 cedis to the pound; the largest note was 500 cedis. So changing £200 to cover all our costs in travelling up-country resulted in receiving a carrier bag full of notes, in tightly packed wads. When we stopped to fill the minibus with fuel, I quickly discovered it was a great time-saver to start counting the money as the fuel was going in; but there was no way I could keep up with the spinning numbers on the pump. The attendants had the benefit of a great deal more practice: the speed with which the notes were counted was phenomenal; the quickness of the hand deceived the eye.

The team, and the wads, arrived at Kaneshi market. We were making another harvest video, investigating the reality and prospects of drought and famine in the continent under the title *A Harvest for Africa?* The plan was to visit a bustling city market, packed with food, and for me to introduce the programme by pointing up the contrast between this vision of plenty and the stereotype of the famine-stricken continent. This was to be my first attempt at a 'piece to camera'; but it couldn't be too difficult, surely – people do them all day on the television.

It all started well. We had tried once, and been sent away to get a permit: the market was private, but if we returned with a government permit, they would be delighted to help us. Now we had the permit. We also had the location, a footbridge over the road with a bird's-eye view of the market, which was indeed packed with food and people, extremely colourful, vibrant, bursting with atmosphere. I thought what I wanted to say; I muttered it over to myself, tried it this way and that. It was only a couple of sentences, but I wanted to get it right.

As Trevor and Derrick got into position, I realised the first problem. The height given by the bridge also meant we were catching the breeze. My hair! The wind was blowing the wrong way. My embryonic Bobby Charlton wisps would be standing on end. *Vanity of vanities, all is vanity, says the preacher*. I had not thought I was quite so concerned about how I looked. Lots of locals, young and old, also seemed curious about how I looked. They began to crowd around, inevitably drawn to this potential pantomime. We were not exactly inconspicuous, up on a bridge complete with my hair, Sally's hair, Derrick's shorts, Trevor's camera.

Still, the market-owners had promised to help, and a number of their security guards appeared. They looked reasonably officious, carrying long canes, but they were on our side. The crowd still built up, and by the time I began my first-ever 'camera, action . . . go', I found myself trying to remember the words, forget the feel of the wind in my hair, and ignore the guards beginning to push people back and threatening to use their canes.

I felt that the sound of thuds and shrieks in the background might be a slight distraction to the viewer; it certainly would be for me. I was not convinced by the first take or the second; but I didn't think getting it right was more important than preserving the bones and skulls of the local children, so I thought it best to quit while I was ahead, or more accurately, while they still had theirs.

Sally was most encouraging, telling me it was OK. It was only when we returned I discovered there had been one other problem. I looked incredibly pasty-faced. A colleague who saw an early version of the programme asked whether anything could be done to put a bit of colour in my face. Sally and Helen did their best, but were forced to report that it could only be done if the background disappeared completely. It was a new twist on the white man's burden.

Trevor and Derrick moved into the market itself and set about gathering shots of the stalls and the produce. It was a photo-opportunity at every turn, but after a few minutes some policemen arrived and insisted we accompany them to the station. We were marched into a dingy office, seemingly crowded with people, some of whom we assumed were policemen. We produced our permit, and gave it to the important-looking man behind the desk. We had no idea how serious our situation was; neither had we any idea how serious Derrick thought his situation was. He was wearing his shorts, a fact he was reminded of when he felt a hand on his thigh; it was a hand that appeared to belong to a policeman, a policeman intent on following his own line of enquiry. Derrick was therefore the most relieved when the permit apparently did its job, and we were released.

It was time to get out of Accra and head north. The next stop was a farm and a farmer. Tom Ahima was no ordinary farmer. He had been Ghana's first 'farmer of the year', honoured on national television. Like Florence, he was also part of Tearfund partner RURCON, a network of Christian agricultural advisers who gave their time to encouraging improvements in food production across Africa. Tom was an extremely successful farmer, but he was committed to sharing his skills and enthusiasm, particularly to encourage talented people to believe that farming was an honourable and commercially viable profession. Over 90 per cent of Africa's agricultural graduates become urban-based civil servants; Tom is still working to change that situation. He is living proof that the gospel which teaches the right use of wealth is essential to true development; otherwise we simply swallow the lie that economics is all, and see wealth replace poverty as the source of misery.

His contribution to our video was important, fighting the stereotype of the African as the helpless famine victim and demonstrating that good harvests were not impossible. We videoed rainfall, sunset, crops growing, crops being harvested, food being prepared, food being eaten. We went into the local village to illustrate Tom's positive involvement with other local farmers. Once again the children crowded round, making Trevor's job almost impossible. So once again it was distraction time. This time I had more space, so I became a Pied Piper, leading over a hundred children a merry dance right down the main street and back again. I discovered they would do almost anything I suggested! Given this power, I can report I limited it to various counting games and generating an enormous shout to accompany a punch of the air. Even now, I can tell you are impressed by this level of commitment and skill.

We thoroughly enjoyed our brief time with Tom, but we needed to press on. It was Derrick's wedding anniversary, so we sang him a song at breakfast, and promised to laugh at some of his jokes. The minibus sped up a good road as far as Tamale, so the afternoon experience came as something of a shock. The road practically disappeared. A few chunks of tarmac were marooned as islands, often several inches above the solid hard-packed red African soil; there was also a series of potholes, some several feet deep. James, our driver, had to make one crucial choice after another: did he go round this hole, or down into it? When it rained it got worse, because when a pothole is full of water, you have no idea how deep it is. Our progress slowed. It took about four hours to do twenty miles. We had expected to make Burkina Faso that day; halfway through the afternoon, James explained he would be unable to drive after dark in Burkina Faso, because he had no orange covers for the headlights. The empires strike back: Burkina Faso has French driving laws, and Ghana British.

We had now spent more hours than we cared to think about sharing the limited space and facilities of the minibus. Derrick's jokes and my snoring had become less entertaining by the hour. Still, there was always music. James had one cassette tape. He liked it. The sound system was not brilliant, but you could recognise the songs. Chris Rea's 'Road to Hell' seemed not entirely inappropriate, but before this trip I had never heard George Michael's 'Careless Whisper'; now I had heard it so often it was infiltrating hidden corners of my brain. When anyone mentions Ghana, I can immediately hear the strains of 'I'm never going to dance again'. Every time it came round, we shrieked it out in unison with ever-growing signs of hysteria.

The next morning we made it to the border. The Ghanaian officials spotted my wad and insisted that I could not take 250,000 cedis out of the country – the limit was 5,000. I was given a receipt, and we headed on to the Burkina Faso customs post. They were incredibly laid back, three soldiers playing cards in front of a large poster advertising a Reinhard Bonnke evangelistic crusade. We dutifully filled in the forms, and we set off again. The road was good, and by 2.00 p.m. we had arrived in Ouagadougou.

A great name for a great place! Burkina Faso is one of the poorest countries in the world, fighting a desperate battle against the encroaching Sahara Desert, and yet its capital city revealed some endearing quirks of colonial legacy: women carrying baguettes on their heads like firewood – bizarrely, French flour is flown in to make this possible; there was a wonderful French patisserie in the centre of town – and signs of the fact that Ouagadougou is the centre of the African film industry. In a busy shop near the centre we bought some authentically colourful African cloth – except the label read 'made in Manchester'.

Guibaré was two hours' drive from Ouagadougou, a genuinely African village. In Burkina Faso the different tribes build unique versions of similar elaborate homes – a series of small huts within a mud wall compound. One hut appears to be the man's sleeping quarters, another the wife and children's; each home has its own granary hut, and its own chicken hut. Their villages are very picturesque: women carrying water buckets on their heads past the thatched huts, their colourful costumes standing out against the browns and sandy yellows of the surroundings.

We visited Guibaré on a Sunday, which gave us the opportunity to experience some African worship. The sermon was about prayer, illustrated from the story of Elijah when the drought is broken; there was fervent prayer for rain, and equally fervent prayer for people to be saved. But the highlight of the service was the offering. A bowl was placed on the floor at the front of the church; a drum began to beat, and people shuffled and danced their way to the front to make their gift, many of them actually smiling. I was still trying to come to terms with this culture shock when the full bowl was replaced by an empty one, and the drum started up again. Once again people shuffle-danced up to the front, and once again notes and coins were placed in the bowl. 'What's the second offering for?' I asked our interpreter. The answer left me slightly stunned: 'The first was the tithe; the second is their thank-offering.'

By now the travelling, the heat, the nights on mud hut floors in villages with no sanitation were beginning to take their toll. We still had one last visit to make, out to an area where Tearfund was supporting CAMA Services in a relief and reforestation programme. It was here that I met my first ever water beds, discovering in the home of an American missionary the cool but slightly unnerving experience of a life on the domestic wave. It was also here that we came face to face with the reality of life on the edge of famine.

Tim Albright, our contact and guide, had arranged our close encounter of the Third World kind. First, we were given a demonstration of survival techniques. One lady led us on a walk out of the village, across a blisteringly hot piece of open ground. The desperate hunt for firewood had seen the forest edge move further and further away from the homes, but among the trees she showed us how leaves and berries were collected. A man demonstrated how he would follow a vine shoot back to the point where it emerged from the ground, then dig down about one metre to find the root. It was hard to believe the energy expended in the search and the digging would be replaced by the calories in the root that emerged.

Back in the village we watched these items being prepared. Some of the berries were poisonous, and had to be boiled several times to make them safe to eat. Eventually a family sat down on the ground around a cooking pot, a plastic bowl in front of each member. A sticky, grey, leafy dollop was put into each bowl. It looked disgusting, severely unappetising. There was a pause; eyes were closed and grace was said. As I looked at the food, it gave a whole new meaning to the idea of saying grace: *for what we are about to receive, may the Lord make us truly grateful.*

We were introduced to the *préfet*, the local government official. He explained to us that the local people, Muslim and animist alike, had asked that the church take responsibility for the famine relief distribution, because they were the only people they trusted to do it fairly. Rene Drabo was one of the elders of the church; Herb, the local missionary, whispered to me that

Rene's method of building that trust was to take less than his own share.

Rene's home was another collection of mud huts within a compound. He took me over to his granary hut. It had a small high hole as an entrance; two wooden handles were built into the wall just above the hole so that Rene could swing himself up and through to get in. Inside, there was nothing. Two years before there had been floods, which had washed away his crops; last year, he had been just about to harvest, when the sky had darkened and a swarm of locusts had descended. When they moved on two days later, there was nothing left. This year, he explained, there had been drought. Just then a donkey entered his compound pulling a small cart. I asked what a good crop would be, in terms of sacks of grain on the cart. 'In a good year,' he replied, 'I would load the cart fifteen times.' 'What about this year?' I asked. 'I only managed to harvest enough for one-third of a cart-load.' His face was impassive, he sat very still, while his children played around his feet.

I had one last question. 'You are a Christian. When you have experienced floods, and locusts, and drought – do you think the Bible is right when it says that God provides for his people?' My questions were being translated into French, then from French into Rene's local African dialect. It was a slow process. It was almost as if my question was hanging in the air, while it got to him and his reply was returned to me. Eventually it came: 'I know that God does not abandon his children, and I know that God does not abandon me. God provides wild fruits for us, God has his eyes on us.' Sometimes I feel that while we might share the same Christianity, it is hardly accurate to say we share the same faith.

The next morning we witnessed the grain being distributed. A man led his blind mother up to receive her portion. These people were visibly poor, living on the edge. They carried the sacks away on their heads, their backs stiff and straight with a solemn dignity. I attempted another piece to camera, designed to offer an ending for the video. There were no crowds to deter me, but my sense of inadequacy went beyond my lack of televisual expertise. As we watched the queue gradually disperse, I turned to Herb, who had worked here for thirty years, and asked him how he felt. He started to choke up. 'These are my friends,' was all he said.

That same day we travelled back to Ouagadougou, and then on to the Ghanaian border. The receipt worked, and I regained my cash. The next morning we negotiated the road to hell through torrential rain and dust-storms. We kept going. At 7.00 p.m. we were going to stop, but the crew now had a desperate desire to leave the minibus, complete with George Michael, behind them for ever. We reached Accra at 11.00 p.m. – 500 miles in one day. We were shattered. It seemed just possible that we were indeed never going to dance again.

16

This is My Body

*The bread we break: when we eat it, we are sharing in the
     body of Christ.
Because there is the one loaf of bread,
all of us, though many, are one body,
for we all share the one loaf.*

1 Corinthians 10:16–17
(Good News Bible)

Human powers of recovery are remarkable. Within three months
Sally, Trevor and Derrick were prepared to risk travelling with
the chief once again. Mind you, the chief had learned his lesson.
This time we were joined by Paul Clark, a professional television
news presenter. Paul is another travelling companion who has
become a good friend. He is a respected presenter and journalist
with Ulster Television, a well-known and well-loved personality
in Northern Ireland. It has been entertaining to see him
surrounded by autograph-seeking Irish schoolgirls at the luggage
carousel in Heathrow, while bemused English bystanders wonder
who on earth he is. The party was completed by Jim Loring, who
was making his first overseas visit as a freelance photographer.

Twenty-one hours after leaving home we were in a dormitory
in the Valley of Blessing outside Sao Paulo, Brazil. The next
morning we awoke to a cold wind and pouring rain, not quite
what we had expected. The Valley of Blessing was more than we

expected. It was the headquarters of the Antioch Mission, founded by Jonathan Santos and one of the leading agencies in the new Third World mission movement which has been such a feature of the end of the twentieth century. Brazil has been at the forefront, its evangelical population, estimated at over 15 per cent of the total, spilling out thousands of missionaries across the world.

So the Valley of Blessing housed the training centre and the twenty-four-hour prayer room, where there was always someone interceding for the world; but it was also the base for a rescue and rehabilitation programme for the street-children of Sao Paulo. Young volunteers from Tearfund's summer teams had helped to build the simple dormitory blocks which housed some of the youngest children discovered abandoned on the streets. Jonathan and his team worked to encourage families to adopt these children; that first morning we interviewed a couple who were adopting Allessandro, a young lad, full of beans, who was clearly excited about the whole process. It was not entirely surprising. We were able to join in his leaving party: cakes, balloons and pop – and a prayer – to celebrate his adoption into a new family.

This was a little like beginning at the end of the story. As we explored the reality of street-children in Sao Paulo it was good to have these seeds of hope planted in our minds. Pastor Fortunato was our guide to probably the second largest city in the world, home to around twenty million people. We were keen to get an overview, and he arranged for us to video from the roof terrace on the top of the House of Italy, the tallest building in the city. We shot up forty-one floors in the express lift, and stepped out. There was a waist-high parapet between us and the completely awesome view.

Straight ahead there was a forest of skyscrapers, stretching away to the horizon. To the right the scene was repeated; to the left, the same again. After a minute, I had to sit on the floor and allow the parapet to block the view. For the first and only time in my life, the sight was too much, it was overwhelming. When I was able to face it again, I was able to take it in a little more: the helicopters buzzing around, urban dragonflies seeking sustenance among the skyscraper reed bed; the swimming pool on the roof of the Hilton Hotel; the glimpses of the streets between the buildings.

The streets: Pastor Fortunato explained that the estimate was that one million children spent their day on the streets, and the majority of them the night as well. He had been a bank clerk; the needs of the children had challenged him to the point of moving his own family into one bedroom so the other could be freed for four street-children to be taken in. This was not enough. He had given up his job so that he could work with the needy full-time, driven by the urgency of the task to try and make a difference.

From the heights to the depths. Part of his parish was to be found under a massive flyover which supported a five-lane motorway; on either side the area was defined by railway lines, where trains bursting with commuters rumbled by every few minutes. It was cold and damp and murky. As we entered the area we could see a rubbish dump with a fire smouldering smokily away; we were greeted by a man who appeared to be drunk, who assured me he was Arnold Schwarzenegger and asked me how Hollywood was doing. Nearby there was a rickety bed in the open, and the man with one leg lying on it welcomed us to the *favela*.

The houses were makeshift, put together from plywood packing cases, pallets, cardboard boxes and polythene. One seemed to be occupied by a family of children; the story seemed to be that a thirteen year-old and her younger sister were looking after their three babies. The whole scene was one of dysfunction and debris. Fortunato led us over to some garage doors hanging drunkenly on to a building that looked at ease in its shanty surroundings. He opened the doors, to reveal a few rows of benches and a ramshackle lectern at the front: this was his church.

I often think of it when I am preaching on a Sunday morning; my act of worship is one I share with those desperate people in the Sao Paulo *favela*, as well as the Indian community in the open air in Paraguay. The world-wide body of Christ has many members.

In the main square of the city we visited the little base that had been set up to act as a contact point for street-children. We saw some, but they quickly melted away as we approached. As night fell the police cars cruised the area; this was where some of the police had decided that treating the children as vermin to be shot was the best approach. It was not surprising that they stayed out of sight. But not far away, reassured by the known and friendly faces of our guides, some were prepared to talk to us. I don't remember much of their conversation, more the haunted, hunted eyes and the plastic bags containing a few drops of nail varnish remover from which they constantly sniffed lungfuls of chemical encouragement.

Our itinerary just said Sao Paulo to Salta, northern Argentina, via Buenos Aires; a simple transfer from the international flight to the internal flight, ninety minutes to do it. It all seemed straightforward. I am not sure exactly when we realised that the international flight came in at one airport, and the internal flight left from another; little did I know that this was to be, in the eyes of some of the team at least, my finest hour.

First we waited for the luggage, desperately willing it to appear on the carousel, which insisted on doing its impression of the watched pot that refused to boil. Eventually it came, and we rushed out to the taxi rank, figuring this must be the fastest transfer option. They were enormous black limousine taxis that turned out to have minuscule boots, so we ended up hiring three and moving into Buenos Aires in a mini Presidential motorcade. Our haste was in weird contrast to the Sunday afternoon leisure of the city. The sun was shining, kites were flying, people were strolling – and our convoy was weaving in and out of the traffic as if engaged in a private taxi grand prix.

The second airport was in the city centre, on the banks of the River Plate. We arrived fifteen minutes before the scheduled departure time. The taxi drivers were prepared to take dollars in payment, but when we dashed up to the check-in we discovered there was an airport tax to be paid, and it could only be paid in local currency. Where was the bureau de change? The other end of the airport building. I ran. The others did not believe I had it in me. I'm not sure I did. I certainly did not have it in me by the time I had finished. It was a hundred-metres dash. I changed the money, and ran back to the check-in desk, the clock ticking away.

'Have you paid the tax, sir?' 'Where do I do that?' 'There's a little office just by the bureau de change . . . ' 'You might have told me,' I yelled over my shoulder as I dashed off again. There was a queue. I hopped from foot to foot, gulping in air, before belting off for one last high speed run. I skidded to a halt at the check-in desk, clutching the tax receipts. The clerk remained completely stony-faced. Presumably that was because he knew the plane was delayed. I need not have run after all. But I had impressed my colleagues.

We eventually took off in what appeared to be a brand new plane, being flown by Austral, a brand new privatised airline that was clearly out to impress. Champagne was served with the meal, then they announced that the pilot would be drawing the winning boarding card, the prize a free flight for two to Mar del Plata. Since none of us had a clue where Mar del Plata was, we did not pay a great deal of attention. Then we heard the name of the lucky winner being announced: Derrick. Hurried conversation resulted in a cunning plan being hatched. We suggested to the stewardess that they should redo the draw, but we would appreciate the opportunity to video in and from the cockpit of the plane.

Which is why Terry Tearaway was later to be seen on the flight-deck of a plane heading towards the sunset over the Andes. The view was spectacular and the pilot very amenable. He showed me how all the warning lights worked, and then produced a brochure and began trying to sell us fishing holidays in Patagonia. We landed after dark and were met by Chris Hawksbee, last seen in Paraguay and now working in the Argentine side of the Chaco. He drove us away in his open-backed pick-up to a restaurant where he ordered a steak for us. We were a little nonplussed until it came, when we discovered it was the size of a Sunday joint and easily fed the lot of us. We were back in the land of the meat-eaters. A remarkable day ended with us standing in the back of the pick-up, all hyped up with tiredness and whooping at passers-by. The streets were filled with election banners exhorting the citizens to vote for Randon P Gonzales. Sally decided she had discovered my secret identity. I became Randon P for the rest of the trip.

The Argentine Chaco was every bit as remote as in Paraguay. We travelled for hours in the pick-up, very hot, very dusty, very little change of scenery, very few people. Chris was doing similar work here, still spending time with family groups, offering support and advice when asked. The highlight of the visit came in Three Bottle Tree village, which was named, surprisingly, after the three distinctive bottle-shaped trees in the village. We were there to witness the bee-keeping project, where Chris was trying to turn a traditional practice into a small commercial concern.

The Chaco Indians had always searched for wild honey in the bush; now they were being shown how to tame the process. First, catch a swarm of wild bees; next, identify the queen bee; clip her wings and keep her in a tiny cage in the hive. When the whole swarm has settled into the hive, release the queen so she can lay eggs. Provide credit for the purchase of hives, protective gloves and veils, and the 'smokers', which blow smoke at the bees to dissuade them from stinging you. Finally, sell the honey, which is now recommended by the local hospital, and repay the loan.

It was agreed that Trevor and Derrick would video the hives. They emerged from the nearby hut looking like extras from *The X-Files*, complete with white hat/veils and gloves, and trying to work out how to operate their equipment in this mode of dress. The hives were in a thicket on the edge of the village. We watched them plunge into the bushes and disappear from sight. Next we knew was a few minutes later, when an angry bee emerged, made straight for Jim Loring and stung him. The angry bee was shortly followed by Trevor and Derrick and several more angry bees.

Paul Clark appeared to be enjoying the whole experience. I was now discovering the secret of the piece to camera done by the expert. Two things seemed to be essential. First, the powder. Paul was not going to risk the pasty-face problem – he had brought his make-up with him. Second, the ear-piece. Paul made sure he said what he intended to say by recording it into his dictaphone and then playing it back to himself as he looked and spoke confidently into the camera. He was used to this system, of course, being professional. What's more, he was so professional his hair did not seem to blow in the wind. I was deeply impressed.

On to Lima. Our video was intended to capture the whole range of the work of Tearfund under the title *Good News to the Poor*. Urban and rural, children and communities, Tearfund workers and national partners, agriculture and small businesses, relief and human rights – locations, projects and stories: in Lima we got them all. We also got Gordon Davies, Tearfund's Latin America manager, quickly and affectionately named and known to Sally as OMIP – Our Man in Peru. He seemed completely unfazed by the team, regarding our moments of strange behaviour and quirky humour with a wry smile of avuncular detachment. He knew Lima well, and, we were to discover, he knew where to eat.

Paul was the one who dared to ask why the streets of Lima had so many people selling calculators. As you drove past, calculators were held out to you; as you walked down the street, they were pushed under your nose. They were actually selling money. Lima was the city of the legal black market for currency exchange, Peru the land of hyper-inflation. Not long before, new bank-notes had been issued: one new *inti* equalled one million old *soles*. It would have been funny if it were not so serious. Fujimori had been elected on the promise of not instituting the austerity measures being demanded by the International Monetary Fund. Within weeks he had broken his promise, and the economy was being brought under control, but at a price: Tearfund's partner CONEP, Peru's Evangelical Alliance equivalent, estimated that 60,000 children had died as a result of the instant jump in food prices.

I still regard Lima as one of the most extraordinary cities in the world. For ten months of the year the sun hardly appears, but it hardly ever rains; and buildings are taxed according to the number of storeys they have; as a result, it was common to see buildings unfinished, with twirls of metal reinforcement sticking up out of the concrete waiting for the roof or the next storey: if you weren't sure, neither was the tax-man. The overall impression was of a building site, grey and unfinished.

Then there was the enormous spread of shanty areas on the edges of the city, stretching out along the grey sand dunes for mile after mile. Vast numbers were pouring into Lima – at one point it was estimated the city authorities should be providing a new school every day. A shanty begins with an invasion – a piece of land identified by a group of squatters, who move on to it *en masse* and begin to build makeshift homes. Within a few hours an empty space has become home to hundreds of families. Then follows a period of consolidation which will go on for years. The houses gradually become more sturdy and permanent – we saw walls of plywood being replaced by bricks a few at a time, as they can be afforded. The residents start to lobby for water and sanitation, electricity and lighting. Electricity makes a big difference, not least to the birth rate; apparently television is a great contraceptive.

Leo Smelt was a Dutch missionary who was working in old and new shanty areas. He was convinced that the gospel had to be incarnated in the lives of the followers of Jesus, so he had moved into the shanties to plant churches and work for the well-being of the people. He took us to MiPeru, an older shanty, where we were introduced to the old couple who were the first to move into the area many years ago. As we sat in their tiny house, we could hear an argument from a house nearby, and I suddenly realised that one of the costs of poverty is a complete lack of privacy. Paper-thin walls, crowded houses crowded together.

From MiPeru we headed out to a new settlement, known unromantically only by its location as Panamerica del Norte 39km. The sand dunes were still grey, as was the sky. The makeshift homes were spread out on the sand. Leo had planted a tiny church, and we joined them for a Sunday afternoon communion service, lit by a spluttering kerosene lamp. It lacked the liturgical splendour of the cathedral; it had all the reality of symbolic truth. *'The bread that we share, is it not a sharing in the body of Christ?'* The body was broken to enable a new body to be created, the world-wide body of Christ. In a deep sense, Tearfund is a realisation of communion.

Afterwards we were talking outside, waiting for Leo, when we realised Jim had started to walk over the dunes, way off into the distance, leaving a trail of footprints in the sand. We could just make out that a cross had been set up on the top of a sand-hill across the valley. When he returned about half an hour later, he was breathless with the effort of trudging through the soft sand, but he had got his picture. It was not until we were back in Britain and looking through the hundreds of transparencies he had taken on the trip that we realised just how worthwhile his effort had been, and how dramatic the shot he had taken. It was the sign of a good professional: seeing the possibility and tracking it down.

The result was a *Tear Times* cover, a book cover and a six foot high print that still welcomes visitors to the Tearfund office in Teddington.

The cross is a symbol of triumph and of suffering. We discovered both in Lima. Peru was in the grip of a vicious terrorist war being waged by the Maoist Sendero Luminoso, the Shining Path. In MiPeru there was a shrine marking the spot where a group of soldiers had been ambushed and killed. The electricity regularly failed, the result of the guerrillas targeting the city's power-lines. In the countryside the church was a target, because pastors were an alternative source of local leadership, and often forced to take one side and then risk retaliation from the other.

CONEP had provided a refugee home for pastor and people from the mountains who had been the victims of the Shining Path. Its location was kept quiet, and, even more ominously, we were advised to sit in the middle of the minibus with Peruvians by the windows so as not to draw attention to our presence in the area. We saw the drawings of the children, complete with helicopters firing crayoned machine-gun fire on the houses below. We worshipped with a small group of Indians still in their country costume, who roared out a hallelujah greeting to their fellow-Christians in Britain. And I interviewed Pastor Alfredo Vasquez.

'We were in the middle of a service and I was preaching when the terrorists threw a bomb into the church and came in shooting,' he recalled. 'I was hit in the arm. All around there were screams and shots. I returned to the pulpit and was grabbed and dragged outside. A guerrilla shot me again and as I fell to the ground I shouted "Glory to God." I lay there bleeding as a brother died beside me.'

As he talked he began to untuck his shirt from his trousers, and then displayed a large scar on his stomach. He had preached against violence, and paid the price. He was not the only one. There had been 21,000 deaths. Peru was seeing hundreds of people 'disappear'; CONEP's Tearfund-supported Human Rights and Rehabilitation programme was developing a rapid response system particularly focused on persuading the government to own up to imprisoned pastors as quickly as possible. They were also helping the children traumatised by violence. We met Carmina, just nine years old, who had lost her parents, killed by terrorists who also deliberately shot her in the thigh. She limped over to us, smiling broadly, but not speaking.

On our way back from meeting Alfredo I was asked if we would like to video a cemetery where Sendero Luminoso fighters were buried. I was not quite sure why we would want to, but they had offered. Gordon was not convinced it was a good idea. In the end we decided to make a quick visit, leaving before our presence was noted. The cemetery was a wall with little boxes almost like pigeon-holes; many of the small doors carried the distinctive and defiant bright red hammer and sickle.

We left nervously and quickly. There was an undoubted tension about the whole visit to Lima. It was a compound of our own tiredness, the reality of the violence, the traumatised children – and in addition, every journey was a white-knuckle stomach-churning roller-coaster ride to adventure. Our Jehu-like charioteer was Luis, who drove our minibus with his very own brand of skill and unassuming bravado. It was just a little unsettling to discover that before he became a Christian he had been the getaway driver for a bank robbery gang. How much change does conversion bring – in driving technique? Lima's roads are relatively straightforward – a very basic grid, so that whatever street you are on, there is a crossroads due in a few moments. Luis' method had a gruesome fascination – he would hurtle towards the junction, and as he reached it, he would touch the brake while he judged whether he needed to stop or accelerate. Whatever conclusion he reached, the effect on the passengers was much the same – your head, your whole body, jerked either forwards or backwards.

All the same, there were compensations. The streets

themselves had the richest array of vehicles seen outside a museum. Because there was no rain, there was very little rust. Cars from the fifties were still in use, often patched together, sometimes not. It was not impossible to see VW Beetles, missing several doors and wing panels, fighting for space with vintage Cadillacs. To become a taxi-driver you bought a plastic sign saying 'taxi' and stuck it on your window. One such stopped to pick me up and the door came off in my hand. The driver leapt out and indicated that I should sit down, whereupon he propped the door back in place and encouraged me to hold on to it, or even hold it on, for the course of the journey.

Gordon thought that for our last night we deserved a treat – or perhaps he wanted to celebrate our impending departure. He suggested that we might like to eat at a very special restaurant. I was quite surprised, because Derrick had already caused mayhem at a pizzeria by picking up the ketchup bottle, beginning to shake it vigorously and thus discovering that the last person had left the top loose. An astonishing stream of bright red sauce shot over Gordon and past his shoulder, where it splattered on to the wall, and then slowly began to drip towards the floor, the St Valentine's Day Massacre revisited. But Gordon, man of faith, was willing to risk us somewhere much more refined.

It was called *L'Eau Vive*, Living Water. When the taxi dropped us outside, I suspected a practical joke. The street was deserted, and we were standing next to a very solid wooden door set in an enormously high wall, a little like the entrance to an exclusive Cambridge college. Gordon's taxi then arrived, and he assured us we were in the right place. We rang the bell, and after a pause the door was opened by a nun, who showed us down a Gothic castle corridor to a high-ceilinged refectory.

We were in a convent, run by a French order of nuns, who financed their work with the poor by running a high-quality French restaurant, with the nuns dressing in their national costume to serve as waitresses. It was frighteningly surreal. I sipped my glass of *kir royale* and said to Sally, 'This is Lima, and I am being served French food by a Tahitian nun. Is that right?' She nodded, looking a little surprised. 'Just checking,' I explained. At that moment, four nuns appeared at the top of the steps at the end of the room, turned to face the statue of Mary and, unaccompanied, gave a beautiful rendering of 'Ave Maria'.

17

The Young Ones

I've been to a place everyone should go
I know things now everyone should know
And I have seen love dampened by rain
Rise in the sun and triumph again.

Cliff Richard

Tearfund's twenty-fifth anniversary; Cliff Richard, one of our Vice-Presidents, was again willing to present a video. The whole organisation was working through a focus on the HIV/AIDS epidemic, alerting partners around the world to the challenges and opportunities the disease presented to the work of Christian development. I was keen to see Tearfund use the positive responses of some of our partners to educate and challenge the church in Britain to think about its own response, but I had been concerned that as a theme it would be difficult to sell. There was little point producing good or worthy resources if everyone shied away from the subject. But a silver jubilee video featuring Cliff – that would be much easier to sell. It would be our best opportunity to communicate a vital message that came from the heart of the organisation.

Once again I was working with Tony Neeves and John Muggleton. Cliff was able to allocate one week from his diary – it was our job to make the most of it. He would be travelling with Bill Latham, who had made an enormous contribution as Deputy

Director in Tearfund's early years. It was Bill who had interviewed and appointed me, before leaving to work full-time with Cliff. So the team, which included colleague Barbara Gallagher, went out in advance to make preparations and gather background material, destination Uganda. Uganda was not only relatively simple to reach, with no jet-lag problems to worry about; it was also experiencing a major and devastating AIDS epidemic – and church and nation were facing up to it as nowhere else.

What I had not realised was just how stunningly green and beautiful Uganda is. Its height on the plateau takes the edge off the heat, and the lush vegetation is home to a rich variety of wildlife. Even on our first day in Kampala, the enormous storks were very obvious, flapping their huge wings or sitting perched on a vantage point. Later in the trip we got up early to video dawn on Lake Edward, complete with hippo wallowing in the water; a troop of baboons greeted us at the point where the Equator crossed the road. The people, too, were warm and welcoming. Amin and Obote had tragically left Uganda known only for its suffering and misery; it was good to discover something more, something different, something positive.

We scurried about, meeting people, gathering information and making plans. The diocese of Namirembe in Kampala was a major Tearfund partner, and Bishop Misaeri Kauma was enormously helpful, arranging for us to book in an interview with the Vice-President of Uganda: the Vice-President meets the Vice-President. After my interview of the Vice-President of Peru on the last trip, this was clearly becoming habit-forming.

We were also given generous help by Jeremy McKelvie, an MAF pilot, together with his wife Sherrie. Along with Kampala we were planning to take Cliff to visit the mission hospital at Kagando, and Jeremy agreed to fly Tony and me out to make contact there and reconnoitre the situation. Kagando is situated in the foothills of the Ruwenzoris, sometimes called the Mountains of the Moon. It was a beautiful sunny day, and Jeremy decided to let us see the mountains close up. We could see a glimpse of something white near the summit, and as we got closer we realised it was snow – equatorial Africa in April.

The small plane got closer still, and I decided that as I had no choice I would simply trust that Jeremy knew what he was doing. It was his wife who eventually said, 'Aren't you going a little close?' How comforting to know that husbands and wives in planes are like husbands and wives in cars. I could not actually believe the plane would have room to turn before plunging into the snowy mountainside – but amazingly it did.

It was difficult to come to terms with reality over these first few days, in fact during the whole visit. It was as if there were actually two parallel worlds: one the obvious surface reality – the beautiful country, with smiling children, busy markets, sunshine and friendly people – the other an almost hidden, submerged world of suffering and heartache. One in four adults in Kampala is HIV positive, their life expectancy six months to three years; there are growing numbers of orphans, extended families extended to breaking point; the educated elite is being decimated, the army 90 per cent infected. When this second world was exposed to view, its impact was profound.

As we drove into Kampala every day, we passed a market street where one of the most obvious vendors was the one with a large selection of coffins outside. Paul Bakibinga, then running Tearfund partner ACET (AIDS Care, Education and Training) Uganda, explained that one of the ways the disease was affecting the culture was that people were struggling to give the time to the traditional lengthy funeral rites, that might last three days. It was just happening too often.

We spent a fascinating hour in a college as students were encouraged to consider the impact of HIV/AIDS on their different tribal cultures. Many tribes still practised the tradition that if the husband died, his brother took responsibility for his wife –

otherwise she would be left homeless and landless, as the land reverted to the husband's family. The students admitted that many brothers saw this responsibility as no more than a sexual opportunity, but one which now carried a great risk. They also confessed that the original intention of the custom had been the protection of the widow, and that this could still be accomplished without risk if the brother took on the responsibility without the sexual rewards. It was also curiously if gruesomely reassuring to discover that the practice of using the same knife for multiple adult male initiation circumcisions had been discontinued.

For a day or two we heard stories, we gathered information, we developed our intellectual understanding of the impact of AIDS. We recognised the significance of the government's willingness to face the issue, and also its decision to promote a message of 'one faithful partner for life' as its chief focus for behaviour change, in sharp contrast to the condom and safe-sex message of the British government at the time. All of this was in my head. It reached my heart in Kampala Baptist Church.

John Ekudu was the pastor. He confessed that when he first realised that HIV/AIDS infection was so prevalent that many in his own congregation must also be infected, he went through a period of a few weeks when he felt unable to shake hands at the door as people left the church. 'Then I remembered that Jesus had reached out and touched the person with leprosy,' he said, 'and I realised that as a follower of Jesus I must share his compassion.' Bishop Misaeri had said much the same thing: 'No one is unclean as far as the church is concerned; the church is a hospital for sinners, and we are all sinners.'

Both had turned their words into action. They had not only begun to speak openly about the disease and its impact, they had started programmes of care for PWAs – people with AIDS. Which was why that particular morning we had arrived to video a women's group at Kampala Baptist Church, who met in a little prayer chapel by the side of the main building. I was acutely aware that I had never, so far as I knew, ever met anyone with AIDS. I had thought about the theology and the principles, I had been perturbed by the unpleasant and unbiblical judgmentalism of some evangelical reactions to the illness – but I had not had to meet anyone facing this particular sentence of death, and in a country which had the barest elements of healthcare available.

As we approached the women round the corner of the church building we could hear them singing: 'God is so good, he's so good to me.' I could scarcely believe my ears. This was one of those moments when I felt a complete pygmy in my faith. These were people whose faith in a loving God was deep and real, or they were most cruelly deluded. I had already learned from John that the church had accepted that their response to those who were HIV positive was not dependent on the reason for their infection. But discovering that some of these women were faithful wives whose legacy from their husbands was to be illness, destitution and early death, made their singing even more remarkable.

For many, the onset of their husband's illness first revealed the reality of his unfaithfulness. It also revealed the possibility that they themselves were infected. Thus they were suddenly precipitated into a maelstrom of emotion and suffering, expected to care for their dying husband in homes with no running water or sanitation, knowing that their husband's death might well leave them homeless, with children to feed and keep in school. Meanwhile they were in an agony of uncertainty about their own condition, with an AIDS test an expensive potential ticket to hopelessness, and every illness perhaps a sign of the end.

These were the people singing of the goodness of God. They gathered for mutual support and encouragement, and to be helped with ideas to generate some income for themselves and their children. As we talked they were sewing a patchwork quilt. One lady backed me to the wall to tell me about her crochet work; or rather, not so much to tell me as to sell me. Her child's education depended on it, she said. She did not need to do much persuading, it seemed the least I could do. I became the proud owner of a set of blue and white woolly table-mats. I still have them. They are not much, but they are a reminder of a group of ladies who within two years were no longer with us.

Perhaps not surprisingly they were slightly nervous of the video camera, but when the crew had packed away they asked me about my family. I produced the photos of my daughters I always have with me, and immediately the atmosphere changed and the conversation began to flow. I was asked their names. When I indicated that the older one was called Katharine, one of the younger members of the group became very animated. 'That's my name,' she told me. 'Do you think I could write to your daughter?' I thought this would be fine, and wrote down my address for her. When I arrived home ten days later Katharine had already received her letter; in fact, she wondered why a total stranger could manage to write when her own father did not seem capable.

I asked if I could read it. It was simply stunning.

I am a born-again Christian and I help with the AIDS ministry of my church. I don't have AIDS but I just wanted to serve God for this time really. I'm on a 6 months' long vacation from junior high school after O levels, which is ending in June. My brother asked me before the vacation began whether I would like to work with the AIDS ministry. I said, 'Yes, why not?' But inside me I was honestly scared.

Very soon vacation began. The day before I began working I just couldn't settle, till I got on my knees and cried before God. I told him, 'God, listen to this, whatever the case may be, you see I'm quite scared of getting involved with people with AIDS, but I have made up my mind that I'll be a sacrifice to you, O God, with my spirit broken and contrite.' I asked the Spirit to empower me to be the best I can to these people.

Right now I'm used to them. I have learned from them and they say they have learned from me. Though there are times which are bad I'm able to cry with them, laugh with them and do things together for the glory of God.

I have read this out loud in churches many times since, and every time I can feel the tingle on the back of my neck: a Ugandan teenager had discovered more about what it means to follow Jesus than perhaps I ever will.

Cliff's arrival made the television news – apparently the Uganda television crew had been waiting for a government minister to arrive when they spotted this vaguely familiar man in shorts. He was glad to arrive at all, the connecting plane having taken off from Nairobi airport tipping Cliff and Bill back into the people behind them, because their seats had not been fastened down. Seeing the TV news revealed to the hotel manager that he had important guests; 'We have been caught with our pants down,' he told me in an interesting use of idiomatic English, and to make up for it, Cliff suddenly found flowers and fruit appearing in his room.

We did not allow him much time to enjoy them. Early next morning we were off to the Bishop, and then Vice-President Kisseka, who turned out to be an eighty-year-old Christian who was delighted to do the interview. Next it was down to Mengo Hospital, and Cliff was tipped into the same experience that we had undergone, except that he was being asked to react on camera as he met people who counselled those who had come to collect the results of their AIDS test, and had discovered the worst.

The next day Cliff visited Bulange, where there was a community base for work with PWAs run by the diocese of Namirembe. The welcome was terrific, a group of ladies singing 'Nobody Knows the Trouble I've Seen' with tremendous and very literal expressiveness. 'Sometimes I'm up,' they sang, straining to stretch their bodies as high as they could, 'sometimes I'm down,' and they crouched down as low as possible. The lead singer particularly was giving it everything she had. Cliff, much to their enormous appreciation, returned the musical compliment, although I could not help feeling that 'The Young Ones' had perhaps been written in the innocence of the days before AIDS – '*So let's live, love, while the flame is strong, because we may not be the young ones very long.*'

The ladies from Bulange went out to visit PWAs in their homes. So we went with them, and Cliff was introduced to Miriam, sixty-five-years-old, gaunt and weak, now bed-ridden, who was clearly near the end. Her room was tiny, and it was difficult to fit the crew into it at all; but the video camera rolled, and Cliff was asked to pray. He held her hand, and prayed clearly and simply: 'Father, we're just here before you, and we're overwhelmed by the love that you show us. Father, thank you for bringing me to this place to meet people like this lady. We pray for her now, Lord, that whatever time she may have left on this earth she may continue to give glory to you and see your love in her life; and we ask you to comfort her now and give her more strength than she has at this moment. We ask this in Jesus' name, Amen.' Every time I have seen the video I have been deeply impressed by Cliff's choice of words in this difficult situation.

Even as he prayed there was a sound of raindrops beginning to beat on the tin roof of the hut, and it quickly turned into a downpour. We were all forced to take shelter where we could, and watch the rain lashing down. It was an experience Cliff turned into a song and recorded on the B side of his next single:

> *Heavens wept – the rains came down*
> *Bulange downpour*
> *The pathway bled – earth turned red*
> *Bulange downpour*

Another season changing,
rearranging
this world of strife.
No shelter strong enough
to carry the weight of life

Someone sleeps with you
Now I weep with you
Bulange downpour
But rain can't ease
your disease
It's just another Bulange downpour

There was just time to video an interview with Paul Bakibinga of ACET as he showed Cliff the main streets of Kampala. Paul had been very helpful, and shared much of his understanding of the possibilities for the church to take a lead in the prevention of AIDS if the traditional reluctance to speak out on sexual behaviour could be overcome in the right way. After all, if behaviour change was the key, then Christians were those who claimed that conversion bringing the power of the Holy Spirit was the best hope for behaviour change. And Paul was able to introduce us to some who had discovered they were HIV positive and had been determined to take their own life, until they had met with Jesus Christ and decided to spend their remaining months helping others to avoid the illness.

As Cliff strolled down the street with Paul, several passers-by looked closely, slightly puzzled, obviously sure they had seen him somewhere before. Cliff had never been to Uganda previously, but one or two older ladies almost secretly confided that they had seen his films on television. One very wrinkled lady smiled broadly, pointed, and exclaimed, 'You are the Bachelor Boy!'

This time it was a man who recognised him, and John's camera angle picked up the whole episode beautifully. He slowed, he stared, he stopped and shook Cliff's hand. 'How are you?' said Cliff, obviously used to being accosted by total strangers. 'You'll be Cliff Richard,' said the man, anxious to confirm the accuracy of his eyesight. 'Thank you for recognising me,' agreed Cliff, which prompted the man to lose his flow. 'I saw you on the . . . ' His voice faded, and he made a square shape with his hands, like a cricket umpire asking for the television replay, and then walked on. Then behind Cliff's back you could see him stiffen, pause, and come running back. 'Can I have a photo?' he said. Cliff put an arm round him, pointed at the video camera several metres away, and told him to smile. He did so, and then went off, obviously happy. I have always wondered how long it was before he realised he was never going to see his photo.

It was time to move on to Kagando. That was easier said than done; moving the team plus the equipment was a quite a major exercise, and so we needed to book two MAF planes for the short flight, plus another small commercial aircraft. This gave some unexpected bonuses: MAF rarely had the opportunity for one plane to be videoed from another in the air, and I could tell that the pilots were enjoying the slight change from routine and the opportunity to do some formation flying.

I was assigned, with the baggage, to the additional plane; I have learned over the years how to handle rejection. Guy, the pilot of the two-engined Piper, was all English public school, and assured me there would be 'no probs'. He was right. It was stunning. It was a beautiful day, the green of Uganda stretched away beneath us, and I could even trace the railway line doing a complete loop on itself to climb a hill below. The two MAF planes flew in stately formation alongside, occasionally manoeuvring to meet the requests from John Muggleton designing a new shot.

There was quite a welcoming party at the airstrip at Kasese; nothing had been seen like this since an official government visit.

Bonny, the hospital manager was there, along with several of his colleagues; there were also two Tearfund overseas worker families – Chris and Louise Potts and Andrew and Louise Holt. When we arrived at the hospital, there was a welcome from the staff at their customary morning staff prayers, which included an absolutely stunning unaccompanied close harmony choir. Their voices were so impressive that Steve Shearn, the sound recordist on the crew, recorded them in the hospital chapel one evening, and we were able to use their music as a hauntingly effective soundtrack on the video, and sell it as a cassette. Cliff, of course, once again had to return the compliment, which has led him to accuse me of being the only person to have made him sing before 8.00 a.m!

Cliff's time was running out. We had a day and a half of hectic activity, first around the hospital wards, where the highlight was being shown the premature baby ward. Sylvia Thorpe, a doctor with CMS (Church Mission Society), explained that premature births were common in the area because of malaria, malnutrition or simply too much hard work. Then she carefully peeled back the blanket covering one patient to reveal a tiny scrap of a baby nestled close to its mother's heart. Sarah Maseraka had given birth to Masika two months prematurely; now one week old, Masika weighed just three pounds. In the absence of incubators and other high-tech equipment, the natural warmth of the mother was not only all that was available; Sylvia assured us that the results were every bit as effective.

Then Isaac, the agricultural manager from the hospital, led us on his Tearfund-sponsored motorbike around some of the neighbouring villages, following staff on some of their agricultural extension, healthcare and AIDS prevention work. The sun shone, the hills looked gorgeous, and Cliff continued to interact naturally and helpfully with the bewildering range of people to whom he was introduced. I reflected that it was great to have a celebrity to work with who genuinely believed in the work

183

of the charity, and who was a gifted and natural communicator.

As the sun began to set we sat down on the veranda of the house where Cliff was staying, and I recorded an interview about his involvement with Tearfund over the years, which we were able to issue as part of a cassette incorporating all the songs Cliff had written himself as a result of his visits. After the recording was over, he produced his guitar and sang the embryonic version of the song he had written on this trip. Eight million people watched him sing it, backed by the All Souls Orchestra, on the BBC's *Songs of Praise* for Tearfund's 25th Anniversary, recorded at the Westminster Central Hall. Fewer than eight heard the first performance, very much 'unplugged', but very special all the same. It gave us the title for the video, and memorably captured the experience of travelling with Tearfund.

Sometimes I'm troubled by the things you make me see
But no matter how I feel, Lord,
here I am, send me.

So I leave my world behind me
I enter this domain
I'm troubled by the gulf between us
I can see your sickness
But I don't feel your pain.

Pity's got no power
Compassion has the heart
Jesus, keep me mindful
that it's you who does the giving
and it's we who need to play our part.

18

Twenty-eight Weddings and a Funeral

> *For better for worse,*
> *for richer for poorer,*
> *in sickness and in health,*
> *to love and to cherish,*
> *till death us do part*
> The Book of Common Prayer

We arrived in Mexico City at a moment of high drama and high risk. It was the '94 World Cup, and Mexico were playing their first sudden-death match against Bulgaria. The pilot had been listening to the game, customs officials were watching the game, the porters were watching the game, the arrival and departure screens were tuned into the game; thankfully, air traffic control were presumably still watching their radar screens. It was the second half, 1–1; by the time we had collected our baggage, it was extra time, 1–1. By the time James' hand luggage, complete with passport, had been stolen, the penalty shoot-out was over. Mexico had lost. They were out of the World Cup.

We could see the city was ready for this. Police in full riot gear were lining the streets. We were told there were 30,000 of them But they were the only people on the streets: we discovered they were there in case Mexico had won. The previous match had seen the celebratory fiesta go beyond the limit, as high spirits became drunkenness, and shops were looted and women raped. It was an interesting introduction to a different culture.

James did eventually replace his passport. He was the video director; a former actor in *Grange Hill*, trained in direction by the BBC, and travelling with a full three-man BBC *Panorama*-type crew. Their experience showed. When the immigration forms were distributed on the plane, as always we were asked to give our address in the country. This usually provoked a scramble through my papers and handing round the answer to the whole team, but they all wrote in 'Hilton Hotel' without any comment. It was not that they thought we were staying in the Hilton – just that, confident that every city had one, and no one was going to check the information, it was the quickest way to get the form-filling completed.

We actually stayed in a city-centre *pensione*-style hotel. There was an earthquake-proof public telephone outside, where I could use my BT Chargecard. With Katharine in Uganda on her first overseas adventure, (and meeting her letter-writing namesake) I was keen to call Susan and check all was well. It was . . . and more. She had received a joyful and affirming experience from the Holy Spirit, tears turning to laughter, laughter that had filled the church the following Sunday. So it was standing on a street corner in Mexico City that I discovered that the so-called 'Toronto blessing' had become a Teddington reality – and a reality for me too on my return.

Our hosts were Saúl and Pilar Cruz. They looked after us with splendid care and attention, and day by day, as we met up with them in Jalalpa, the outlying community in which they worked, we uncovered a story that was breathtakingly remarkable and encouraging. Saúl was an intellectual, a lecturer in psychology at Mexico City University, a thinker prepared to turn his thoughts into action. Pilar was a significant catalyst for that process, a woman with friends in high places, always fashionably dressed – those heels really did not seem completely practical for everyday wear in Jalalpa – and determined not to be deflected by difficulty. I have rarely met a couple who so demonstrated that problems really are opportunities!

Saúl had done a survey which revealed that there were slum areas of Mexico City, populated by two to three million people, which had no Christian witness. Two years later they had been together to the Christian Impact course in London, 'The Christian in the Modern World', where I have occasionally had the privilege of taking a morning session. The day they returned, determined to find the right way of living for Jesus in the context of the largest city in the world, they had been guests at a dinner in a church. As the after-dinner speaker Saúl had found himself letting rip on the importance of living and preaching a gospel that was good news to the poor, rather than continuing the middle-class comfortable complacency of church life that was obviously a feature of Mexico City, as in so many other places.

Afterwards Saúl had been taken on one side by an elder at the church, and driven out to Jalalpa. It was a desperate slum area, built on and around a five-fingered ravine with precipitous sides, crowded with people, and lacking sanitation, electricity, proper paths and roads. It was not a wise place to be late at night, either, but to Saúl's amazement the elder said 'What would you do if you could have some land here?' It was not very promising. They were by a steep slope on the edge of the local rubbish dump. Saúl laughed as he told us what his answer had been: 'I would build a Christian Urban Transformation Centre.' He was not even sure what it was, let alone how he would build it, but the man replied, 'Well, you've got it. I am going to donate this land to you.'

For three months Saúl drove there regularly in his car, and sat praying and reading his Bible. One wet grey afternoon there was a knock on his window. A sinister-looking figure wrapped in a poncho, his hat pulled down over his eyes, said, 'I have been watching you. What are you doing here?' Saúl was forced to give a little more substance to his vision of a Christian Urban Transformation Centre. The man listened carefully, then said, 'I like it. But if you ever betray us, you will end up with a knife in your stomach. Is that clear?'

It was Pilar who made the breakthrough from here. Saúl had been reluctant even to tell her about Jalalpa, but now she began to visit regularly, getting to know the children and their mothers particularly. Local people helped to build the initial simple community centre, and the children started to come for homework clubs and other activities. They called the centre Armonia, 'the closest word in Spanish to *shalom*,' explained Saúl. You could tell he had been to Christian Impact.

Pilar discovered the people were concerned about the health risk posed by the complete lack of sanitation. When she suggested that drainage pipes would help, they explained that the local authorities would have to be involved. 'Let's go and see the mayor,' was Pilar's reaction, so the mayor, a powerful local figure, found himself faced by a group of women, one of whom had the novel idea that it was a politician's job to improve the welfare of his citizens. When he realised that the rest of the group were women from the slums, he had the bright idea of suggesting that if they could dig the ditches in one month, he would provide the pipes free of charge. Otherwise they would have to pay. It just so happened that Saúl had a team of volunteers arriving from the United States the next day – the ditches were dug, and the mayor's bluff was called.

One night Pilar did not arrive home at 6.00 p.m. when expected. It was pouring with rain, and Saúl, knowing that floods had washed away homes and killed thirty-one people not long before, became increasingly concerned for her safety. Eventually she returned home at about 2.00 a.m., when Saúl discovered she had been trying to help seventy-three-year-old Doña Mary save her home from being washed away. This left Saúl anxious to avoid risk to Pilar, and Pilar concerned to help her friends. 'You must build them new houses,' she told Saúl, who knew nothing about building houses. But he knew a man who did. He brought a team of volunteers, and they built two sturdy, simple homes to re-house the poorest who lived on the edge of the stream that was an open sewer all the time, and a raging torrent after heavy rain.

Around this time Tearfund became involved, and helped to finance the creation of another forty-nine homes. We stood on the lip of the ravine opposite the community centre, and could see their distinctive red roof tiles, made at Armonia's own income-generating scheme, dotted about on the hillside, standing out among the tightly packed homes. This was the day that we had been scouting about looking for locations to give the impression on the video of how Jalalpa had been before the urban transformation had begun.

We had been down by the side of an open sewer that was still there, some distance from the Armonia building, when James had spotted a group of mounted police approaching. This was a fairly recent occurrence, as Jalalpa had been a no-go area for the police for a long time after some had been murdered. That probably explained why, as we could see when they got closer, they were heavily armed. By now James had stopped them with his best BBC accent, and asked if they would mind being videoed riding past. I was not at all sure about this, being concerned that perhaps they might want to see our permits or ask rather too many questions about what we were doing.

But they seemed happy enough, so they duly took up position, and to a cry of 'action' they cantered forwards and passed the camera, which followed them as they began to climb the road sloping up into the distance. As they did, a car overtook them, and was forced quite close by a bus coming in the opposite direction. One of the horses started, lashing out with its rear feet and landing a solid blow on the passing car, leaving a small but noticeable dent. To my amazement the driver leapt out and began to complain bitterly to the police, and came over to us to insist that we ought to be able to give evidence on his behalf. The next day Armonia even had a message asking if we could provide a copy of the video.

That was not our only video adventure. The area had been extensively mined for building gravel and sand when Mexico City was being built in the 1940s, when Jalalpa was still an area of fields and streams. Now it was honeycombed with tunnels and caverns, some only a few feet from the surface. This had been revealed when the road near Armonia collapsed into a hole several metres deep. Saúl and the community had persuaded the authorities to help build supporting walls underground – this was something we had to see.

There was a padlocked door in the hillside just behind a house. Saúl opened it and led us inside, wearing a natty line in yellow hard hat. After negotiating a lengthy tunnel we set up the camera and some lights, and recorded an interview with Saúl standing next to the wall, built partly with Tearfund's assistance. I noticed that Richard Hanson, our staff photographer, seemed remarkably keen to take his pictures and leave. It was only afterwards that I remembered he was a trained engineer. He obviously knew too much. I would like to claim that my willingness to stay was based upon my spiritual maturity and deep trust in God; actually, I just don't have any imagination when it comes to risk assessment.

The houses certainly met a need, but also revealed the next problem. In Mexican law couples could only be joint owners of the homes if they were legally married. Saúl and Pilar knew that most of the couples who had received the homes were not married – not out of choice, but because they simply could not afford it. They had to pay for blood tests, for the judge to perform the ceremony, and they had to provide a good *fiesta* for friends and neighbours, otherwise they would lose face in the community.

But if they were not married, the house would have to be made over to the man, who, given the right to a new home might well decide that it was time for a new partner to go with it.

Pilar again knew the answer. 'We'll marry them,' she said. They had a doctor friend who did the blood tests; Pilar knew a judge whom she persuaded to donate his services; Armonia provided the building, the cake and the decorations; other churches in Mexico City contributed the wedding rings; and the couples themselves contributed to the *fiesta*. Only one other thing was needed: the official witnesses.

Which was why, for the first and only time in my travels, I had packed my best suit. I had to attempt to look respectable, sit alongside the mayor and his wife, shake hands with every couple and legally witness their wedding. It was an absolutely wonderful experience. The Armonia Centre was packed, full of festivity. On this particular day twenty-eight couples were getting married, bringing the total to 148 – meeting the original need had created a new community service. They came up two by two, all ages, all shapes and sizes. Eduardo and Guadelupe had been together for fifty-one years; one of their children also got married, so their grandchildren had two family weddings the same day!

One of the mayor's bodyguards was obviously either suspicious or confused. I overheard him in animated conversation, and I gathered he was asking about the status of the building – was it a community centre or a church? Apparently this was an important legal distinction, and while the building was registered as a community centre, and the weddings were civil weddings, it clearly also held religious services. The answer to the bodyguard's question revealed a fascinating story.

Saúl and Pilar had opened Armonia, but Saúl had not preached, they had not organised evangelistic meetings – they had simply begun to demonstrate the love of God. After eighteen months the centre was going well, but they had seen no one become a

Christian. The breakthrough came from an unlikely source – the local drunk. Everyone knew him; he was often to be seen reeling down the street past the centre, dirty, sometimes brandishing a knife.

The night he came looking for help he was sobered by the state of his children. He had been short of food, and scavenged some chicken off the rubbish dump. It had not done them much good, and now they were suffering diarrhoea and vomiting on a grand and dangerous scale. Saúl did not hesitate. He bundled them all into his car and set off for the local hospital, where the necessary treatment was obtained. When they had recovered, the father was still sober and sobered. He asked Saúl why he had been willing to allow his car to be messed up for the sake of his children.

'It is because we love you,' explained Saúl. 'Love?' queried the man, 'Why do you say you love me and my family when I have nothing to give you?' 'I'm just representing Jesus,' replied Saúl, 'Jesus is the one who loves you.' 'Jesus?' he said, 'you mean God?' Without another word he went out of his shack, stared into the sky, tears rolling down his face. 'God, I'm sorry,' he said. 'You used to talk to me a lot when I was a child, then I forgot that you were with me.' Saúl was then able to explain to him how he could enter into a new relationship with God, and he became the first Christian in the community.

He realised that he needed to deepen his understanding, and asked Saúl to show him how to learn from the Bible; within three weeks seventy friends were crowding into his tiny house, anxious to join in the Bible studies that Saúl was giving, designed to help people who could not read or write discover the truth of the book for themselves. They overflowed into the street, and the man suggested to Saúl that they should meet somewhere with enough room to get everyone in. 'Where do you think we could go?' asked Saúl. They looked at him slightly puzzled. 'You have built a community centre. Why couldn't we meet there?' they asked.

So when the bodyguard asked his question, Saúl was able to reply that the religious activities that took place there were at the request of the community. There was now a worshipping community in Jalalpa; '*because God has poured out his love into our hearts by the Holy Spirit*' might well have been their own explanation.

We visited one of those red-roofed houses and met Santiago and his mother. She was so proud of him; he was marrying Felicitas at the community wedding. He had been a security guard, and witnessed an armed robbery in which two of his colleagues were shot dead. His mother knew Pilar, and pleaded for their help, convinced that the criminals would come looking for Santiago. Saúl and Pilar arranged secretly for him to go and stay with a friend who was a pastor near the border, well away from Mexico City. While he was there, Santiago became a Christian. When he returned, he had decided he would marry Felicitas before he began living with her. He was the first person in Jalalpa to do this; Felicitas told me that she had been surprised and pleased. It had caused quite a stir in the neighbourhood.

Another of the brides confided to Pilar, 'For the first time in my life I feel clean.' I doubt Saúl quite had this in mind when he blurted out those words just a few years earlier, but it was a heart-warming aspect of Christian Urban Transformation. I asked Saúl to explain the motivation for all their commitment and effort for the people of Jalalpa. He replied, 'Compassion for their suffering; obedience to Jesus Christ, who has sent us to work with the poor; indignation, when we see people created in God's image suffering in this way.' There was now sanitation, electricity, paved streets, children doing better in school, safe housing with security of tenure; there were also children serving big slices of gooey wedding cake to happy couples and their friends and relations. Tony Campolo has a book memorably entitled *The Kingdom of God is a Party*; that day in Jalalpa I shared in a glimpse of the Kingdom.

* * *

Our video for Tearfund Sunday was a focus on urban mission, contrasting Saúl and Pilar's work in Jalalpa, where there had been no church, with Addis Ababa, where there were strong churches. It was a real joy to return to Ethiopia and discover that the fall of the Marxist government had released the church into open and vibrant life. 'I think we're having a revival,' said Ato Berhanu Kebede, who had seen his church, the Geunet Church, grow rapidly over recent months. On Sunday morning we worshipped with them, two thousand exuberant people, in a building which had formerly been a jail where many of them had been imprisoned for their faith. They were running a school for the poorest in the community, supported by Tearfund, its effectiveness so appreciated that local Muslims were asking it to take their children.

At another church we met an elder, in his seventies, who had sold his television so that he could continue to sponsor a child from his own church, and enable him to stay in school. Tearfund's partner Compassion had just begun its child support programme in Ethiopia, building on this local initiative. It was great to see so many children being given the education that meant so much to their parents, and potentially so much to them. We squeezed into a tiny shack packed with tots enthusiastically learning their Amharic alphabet; we interviewed a car mechanic who attributed his employment not primarily to his education, but to his reputation for honesty, gained because through his sponsorship he had stopped being a thief and become a Christian. It was a great affirmation of a proper sponsorship process carried out in a Christian context.

One of our key guides to the new Addis Ababa was Andy Meakins, seconded by Tearfund to the Kale Heywet Church as their urban ministries co-ordinator. I first met Andy in my second month at Tearfund, driving him up to Newcastle for one of our tenth anniversary meetings, where he was to be the guest Tearfund worker, talking about his role as a water engineer in Ethiopia. We had a long and animated conversation, which revealed that despite his quiet and unassuming manner, there was already a deep commitment to his Lord and to Ethiopia.

As we arrived in Newcastle and crossed the Tyne, we did notice that it was snowing quite hard. We were not expecting quite so much snow, however; a few brave souls made it to the meeting, but the next morning we were due to drive on to Glasgow, and the only road open was the A1 going south. By 5 p.m., after a nightmare journey, we were stuck on the M62, and eventually crawled off the ice- and snow-bound road and found a friendly vicar in Leeds who offered his guest bedroom to four slightly hysterical travellers.

So it was good to renew friendship with Andy when we returned to Ethiopia with the video crew. He had continued as a water engineer; it was his team that had been responsible for the capped spring I had seen in 1984. He later returned with a commercial company, and then again with Tearfund; by now he had married Ruth, a remarkable and lovely Ethopian women, and they had three very lively children. He showed us the slums of Addis where he was encouraging the church in its work and witness; he shared his conviction and passion in an interview which belied his natural diffidence.

It was thus a double shock when I received a phone call early one November Sunday morning two years later: an Ethiopian Airlines plane had been hijacked and crashed into the Indian Ocean, and Andy was believed to have been on board. Later that day it became increasingly clear that Andy was not among the survivors, and in a cold and dark Tearfund office I began to send out faxes to the media to indicate that a Tearfund worker was among those missing believed killed. Within minutes I was asked for an interview for Independent Radio News, minutes after that a *Mirror* reporter was at Andy's parents' front door – she happened to live round the corner. I quickly became the contact for all the media to take the pressure off the family, and found myself giving pictures of Andy to motorcycle couriers who arrived all through that Sunday evening.

The next day I was giving television interviews. I could not help but reflect that the only news is bad news. Andy Meakins had given years of faithful and effective service to the people of Ethiopia, and it was only his sudden and tragic death that made it news. Tearfund has rarely had so much media coverage. My only comfort was that at least in his death we were able to honour his life.

At the memorial service in Addis Ababa the reports were confirmed: after the hijack Andy had helped a frightened flight attendant to commit her life to the Lord; she had survived, and reported that as the plane made its final descent, Andy was one of those who had stood and encouraged his fellow-passengers to put their faith in Christ and led them in prayer. At the same service a Muslim man came to express thanks for Andy's friendship to his slum community; quite unbeknown to anyone else, Andy had regularly visited them as he passed on his way home from work, an additional sign of his unstinting commitment to the Lord and to people.

I attended Andy's memorial service in Beckenham, at the church where he had grown up through Sunday School and Pathfinders. A man wearing a clerical collar stepped forward and indicated that he had followed the same route through the church with Andy. Both had subsequently developed that commitment into their career – and he just wanted to thank those unsung heroes who had given their time to children and young people, laying down a grounding of understanding and commitment that had become the bedrock of their lives. That flight attendant and that Muslim man in Addis Ababa were affected by someone whose own life had been shaped by faithful Sunday School teachers. God has his own measurement for hero status. And praise God that in creating the web and weave of the Kingdom of God, we all have a part to play.

19

Condoms and Conversations

And in another land, there's a voiceless cry
Because all humanity sailed on by
They've been betrayed a thousand times
but still the children stand
with no helping hand
Just the knowledge in their souls that it shouldn't be.
Know that you're precious
so precious.

Martyn Joseph

Four babies born every second; the world's population growing at the rate of three Wembley stadium crowds every day. These were the simple facts that lay behind the Cairo UN Population Conference in 1995. The conference itself seemed to polarise around two distinct and opposite views of the significance of those facts. The view represented most forcefully by the family planning/population control lobby was that people are polluters and consumers; the more there are, the more damage they do to the planet, stretching its finite resources to the limit and, some time soon, beyond the limit. In the opposite corner, the Roman Catholic Church, arguing that if God made and makes human beings in his own image, there can never be too many of them; people are a blessing.

This issue (the issue of issue?) raised acute questions for

Tearfund. At the macro level, what impact could genuinely be made on poverty if the numbers of poor people grew at such a rate, population growth now largely being a feature solely of poorer nations? At the micro level, how did and should our partners involved in community health respond to both the pressure and demand for contraception to be widely and easily available? Was there a specifically biblical view of these questions that should shape our policy and communication as an evangelical organisation?

So population became a special corporate theme for Tearfund. We asked Roy McCloughry, an economist and theologian, to bring both these skills to bear, consult widely, help the organisation to think through the issue, and then communicate the conclusions to partners and supporters. The communication dimension was my responsibility, and it was a real pleasure to work with Roy: erudite and with formidable intellectual abilities, yet extremely good company. I did have one advantage, which Roy took more seriously than I – he had never travelled in the so-called Third World. The wise old man of the world was a role I could play with only a minimum of conviction, but Roy was gracious enough to appear impressed.

Roy attended and spoke at the Cairo Conference on Tearfund's behalf, accompanied by Terry Gibson, who was once again charged with directing the video. The plan was to explore the answers to those basic questions by visits to Kenya, one of the fastest-growing populations in the world, and India, about to become the most populated country in the world. The advances in technology, coupled with Terry's own skills, now meant that he could collect video material by himself, using a professional standard camcorder. It certainly made my logistical role a lot simpler.

Tearfund owned a house and a vehicle in Nairobi; this meant we had our own base and our own transport. We could visit a partner and come back via the game park, we could take it in turns to drive and see who could frighten the others the most. We could even miss a turning and drive another fifty miles before we noticed. As a result we had some entertaining highlights: finally finding some giraffes to convince us there was some game in Nairobi Game Park, then also convincing ourselves that we were not going to make the exit before it closed for the night; driving out on to the dried-up edge of Lake Nakuru, where years before I had seen millions of flamingoes and now there were only thousands, and where Roy lost his nerve in the middle of a piece to camera, under the impression he was about to do a David Attenborough and end up knee-deep in guano or worse by disappearing through the crumbling surface of the lake bed.

We set off to visit Stephen Talitwala, the Vice-Chancellor of Daystar University, a major East African Christian educational institution. The plan was to find him at the graduation ceremony, after which we hoped he might have a few moments to spare. That was when we discovered that Daystar had opened a second campus way outside Nairobi; when we eventually discovered its entrance on the main road, the stream of vehicles travelling down its two-mile dirt road driveway suggested we might be a little late. We fought our way through the choking dust, and eventually reached the car park, where there were still one or two family groups standing about chatting. We pulled into the first available space, and I got out to enquire of the nearest person if he knew where the Vice-Chancellor might be found. He smiled, and indicated that he was the very person.

We were able to record a rather snatched but fascinating interview with him and the Chancellor. We rapidly discovered that they felt that the church in Kenya faced a massive challenge. The rapid growth in population was matched by a rapid growth in the church; both were part of a society undergoing massive and rapid change. They explained that the government had recently produced a sex education plan for schools. The church had objected and the government had listened – but what had the church to offer in its place? There needed to be a bold and coherent Christian alternative, coming from a church that spoke out and offered an example and lead on issues of parental responsibility, marriage relationships, sexuality and gender.

This was a view emphatically endorsed by Gladys Mwiti, leader of Tearfund partner Oasis Counselling. She revealed that the spread of HIV infection had encouraged an extensive marketing campaign for condoms. Churches and mosques had been asked to act as free distribution centres; I tried desperately to imagine the discussion of this proposal at a typical church council meeting. It was a salutory reminder that different cultures produce different pressures for the church.

Gladys is a remarkable woman. She was not only developing an almost uniquely African style of individual Christian counselling, but also writing regular columns in leading Kenyan magazines and newspapers. This was a reminder of the significant place of Christianity in the life of the nation, but Gladys was concerned that the solutions being offered to Kenya came from the secular thinking of other nations. She was scathing of the determination of Western governments and aid agencies to impose widespread use of the condom as the answer to the nation's ills, quick to point out that the availability of contraception had done little in Western societies to reduce teenage pregnancy, or to encourage fidelity and proper care and concern for children.

'If the church knows what works,' she said, 'then the church should go ahead and give it. No one has told young people, for example, that self control is a fruit of the Spirit. You can't fill a values vacuum with a condom.' It was the clash of Western values with the collapsing tribal culture that I found so fascinating as we spent time in various conversations with Christian leaders, who obviously felt the challenge of responding confidently and biblically, but also felt the danger of being overwhelmed in the flood. The African tribe viewed children as a blessing; but now, with half the nation under the age of fifteen, the West was teaching them to view children as an economic liability, and the Anglican Church employed diocesan family planning auxiliaries.

If it was fascinating to me, it was a matter of life and death to those involved. We spent just a few hours in Soweto, a relatively new slum on the outskirts of Nairobi. Most of the people had been living in a slum just by the bus station in the centre of the city. For them, urban redevelopment meant waking one morning to the sound of the bulldozer moving purposefully and destructively through their homes. Now they were fifteen kilometres out of the centre, a costly bus-ride from where they made their living, and in an area with no water, sanitation or electricity. Water was a three-kilometre walk; most distressing of all, we were told that when it rained, not only did people save themselves the walk by taking their requirements from the latrine pits that had filled with water, but also that children and old people had drowned after falling into them in the dark.

This was urban reality for many of those who had left their traditional life in the countryside. In a Maasai village, with the sun beating down on the bare earth, a tiny dung beetle rolling a relatively enormous two-inch ball of cow-pat past our feet, and the difficulties of survival being explained to us, we could at least understand why people took the risk of the move. Elsewhere, up in the lush hills of Molo, we spent a more enriching time with a group of women who were working together to grow crops and make the most of their situation.

Gladys had introduced us to them, and she weighed in with the stirring of a massive bowl of mashed potato accompanied by an equally stirring rendition of a song and much chatter and laughter. She also pointed out that these were the women whose husbands had often already left for the city, and whose life had effectively become marginalised from their own family. Sometimes they set up a second family in Nairobi; sometimes their life fell apart. And the women were left to feed and educate the family, and to become the engine for change. Gladys was convinced that the widespread call for the empowerment of women had to be accompanied by a genuine movement to help men discover their purpose and role in a new African culture. In Kenya as in Britain, there were many women who wanted children but who did not want men.

In Kenya we had spent some time at a Christian conference in the hills, where most memorably the Sunday worship had included passionate and tearful intercession for Africa; in India, our visit began with the Oxford Conference on Christian Faith and Economics, which was taking place in the Sheraton Hotel in Agra. This inevitably had a slightly different feel. The conference was an extension of one in Oxford, which was trying to establish whether there was a particular Christian view of economics; Roy was deeply involved, and the conference seemed a good place to begin our further exploration of population issues in what is probably now the country with the most people in the world.

There were a large number of Americans at the conference, many of them ardent proponents of the free market. Their clash with those who felt the living conditions of thousands just outside the marbled walls and halls of the Sheraton might just suggest a weakness in the ability of the free market to deliver health and happiness to all generated a lot of heat, but also, thankfully, a little light.

One of those Americans was a kind of young genial giant, six foot five, in well-pressed shorts from which tree-trunk legs emerged. He was E. Calvin Beisner, Associate Professor of Interdisciplinary Studies, Covenant College, Georgia, the author of a book which revealed a free market thinker who did care about poverty and also attempted to take the Bible seriously. 'I see people as a blessing rather than a curse,' he explained. 'I see a growing population as good news, not bad news. After all, population doesn't grow unless fewer people are dying than are being born and life is generally a good thing, so I think population growth is a good thing.'

We also met Dr Raja Chelliah at the conference. He offered a sharp contrast in views and in physical appearance. He was a diminutive elderly Indian Christian who was Fiscal Advisor to the Indian Government. He gave us permission to interview him in his office in Delhi, so much to our delight we were able to enter the monumental seat of government, designed by Sir Edwin Lutyens and bequeathed by the Raj. Dr Chelliah had an enormous office that matched his enormous responsibilities, with an enormous desk accompanied by a leather chair into which his Lilliputian figure almost seemed to disappear. He was clearly proud of the economic advances India had made, and was convinced that primary education, particularly of girls, and the improvement in the status of women generally, would undoubtedly accelerate the trend towards smaller families.

The highlight of our stay in Agra was going to see the Taj Mahal at dawn. We set out at 6.00 a.m. in tiny rickshaw taxis, being taken round to the other side of the river for the view the tourists do not usually see. It was magical. A camel drooped lugubriously by; then beautiful birds added almost the only movement to the scene, apart from a small boy collecting water from the river, performing his routine chores oblivious of the awesome reflection before him. The marble splendour rose majestically across the water, pink-tinged by the rising sun. It was breathtaking.

It was also a massively ironic comment on our project. Not just a fabulously lavish monument to one woman in a nation of one billion people; Roy had discovered that Mumtaz Mahal had died giving birth to her fourteenth child. Wealth might create a memorial; it cannot ultimately protect from the realities of life, realities shared by rich and poor alike.

* * *

We met the poor in the Delhi slums, the *bustees*. Our guide was Dr Kiran Martin, another remarkable woman, director of Tearfund partner ASHA – Action for Securing Health for All; *asha* is also the Hindi word for hope. A brilliant newly qualified doctor, the world at her feet, she began with little more than a determination to serve the poor, a table and chair in a needy *bustee*, and a plan to train the slum-dwellers themselves as health-workers.

From these inauspicious beginnings she has negotiated with political leaders to win land-rights for the slum-dwellers; she has obtained sanitation – we met some of her health-workers in a clinic on the second floor of a sixty-seater toilet block – and even persuaded the authorities to rebuild some *bustees* entirely, complete with brick homes, paving, electricity, water supply and sanitation. The impact has been dramatic: malnutrition has virtually disappeared, infant mortality is almost eradicated. Now she is on government committees for urban healthcare, and ASHA is asked to take on more slum communities: when we visited she had trained health-workers in twenty-two *bustees*, caring for 180,000 people.

She told us the story interspersed with captivating giggles which seemed to reflect something of her own enjoyment and diffidence that God had chosen to use her this way. The giggles grew with her excitement at telling us how some of the people had responded to a special Christmas presentation of the gospel by Indian evangelists who had come and spent time in the *bustees*: now there was a church established as a result.

As she showed us round, we could see that Kiran was obviously held in great respect. That was why she was able to gather a group of around thirty women, and allow us to ask questions about their attitudes to children and family planning. It was a happy occasion, the women in their bright saris laughing and giggling at our questions and their friends' answers. I was less sure what the children made of it, as they heard their mothers explain that one or two children was quite enough. Kiran assured me that we had probably talked about things with them that they had never discussed with their husbands; but then I think it is the only time I have talked to a group of women about my vasectomy (which I had in a maternity hospital: presumably revenge is sweet).

We met Kala Devi outside her tiny home, where she lived with her husband and seven children. I plucked up the impertinence to ask her how they all managed to sleep – the room was only slightly larger than the bed, and the only other space was a kitchen extension that had room for one person and the fire. She explained that two slept on the bed, two in the three-foot gap between the end of the bed and the wall, and three under the bed. She and her husband slept on the pavement outside. When I asked the women what they wanted most, they had said, 'Electricity'; when I asked what they wanted electricity for, to my surprise they said, 'Fans'. When two months after our visit I read in the paper that the temperature in Delhi had touched 130° F, I remembered Kala Devi's sleeping arrangements.

Despite this situation, and despite the fact that she was once again pregnant, Kala Devi had a contented smile. All her seven were girls; now she knew she was having a boy. The day she had received this news, she had celebrated by buying sweets for her daughters and her neighbours. She had been for an ultrasound scan. Kiran Martin explained the reason was simple. A boy is a security for his parents' old age, effectively their old-age pension; a girl is potentially a liability, with the outlawed dowry still often being exacted as a bride price. That was why there were advertisements suggesting that a few rupees now could save thousands later: the price of the scan and abortion being set against the cost of the dowry. That was why there were some Indian villages with no girls under the age of five. That was why shortly after our visit, the Indian government outlawed the use of ultrasound scans for determining the gender of the unborn baby.

* * *

I doubt whether the village of Barod exists any longer; they told us it was due to disappear under the reservoir created by a new dam. It was, no doubt, just a village like hundreds of thousands of others. We wanted to ensure our investigation of population allowed for the rural as well as the urban, which is why Dr Bachan of the Emmanuel Hospital Association had taken us from his base at the hospital in Lalitpur to see a rural community health-care programme in action. The health visitor was dispensing vaccinations to squealing babies; Dr Bachan was carefully examining an old man who had unwound his turban with a dignified but weary movement.

Baijanti was large with child; the nurse listened carefully with her foetal stethoscope. Her first child was given his injection, his determination to cry competing with his fascination with the video camera. Baijanti was twenty, and had been married for nine years. She was convinced she should have no more than three children, even though most people in Barod had five or six. To her it was obvious: fewer children meant the chance of a better education and a better chance in life.

The next morning we returned early to video Baijanti at work. She sat in the back of the ox-cart as it rumbled slowly out into the fields, where, seven months pregnant, she was to spend the day squatting in the hot sun harvesting chick peas. After half an hour we were out in the country, no one in sight. It could have been the least populated country in the world by the evidence of our eyes. There was so much space; time seemed to stand still.

We came back, Terry to produce the video, me to write resource material for churches to use on Tearfund Sunday, Roy to complete a booklet on a Christian view of population issues, and to draft a population policy document for Tearfund. We felt that all three of us could communicate a genuinely biblical 'third way', that fully affirmed that children are a blessing, and deserve the opportunity to experience life as a blessing; that families should be the place where informed decisions are made about family size; that the responsible use of appropriate methods of family planning within marriage should be promoted alongside education about healthcare enriched by moral values that celebrate life and human relationships. We did not want to forget that the challenge of population growth was also a challenge to consumption growth in the industrialised world.

But among all the words, the policies, the conversations, the debates, Terry produced the image which captured the heart. Baijanti, in a richly coloured orange sari, sat silent outside her mud hut, unmoving, reflecting on her hopes for her children. As a solitary butterfly flutters by, on the soundtrack Martyn Joseph's poignantly simple song expresses the profoundest truth: 'know that you're precious'. I had a letter a few months later telling me that both Kala Devi and Baijanti had given birth to healthy baby boys. Two more of the six billion. And every one precious.

20

Entering a War Zone

To build up cities an age is needed,
but an hour destroys them.

Seneca

I met Terry over breakfast in Garfunkel's, Terminal Four, Heathrow – the latest shopping mall in west London, which so successfully gathers together under one roof everything you don't need and are glad you haven't got the money to buy. Then on to a brand new Boeing 777, which provided an air travel novelty in having comfortable seats, helpfully cushioned head-rests, overhead lockers you could not bang your head on, and individual video screens in the back of the seat in front. Add to that your own personal telephone – all you needed was your credit card and $8 a minute – and what more could one ask? We even arrived at Dubai on time. The wonders of modern technology.

We refrained from buying a Dubai duty free lottery ticket, price $139, prize a big BMW. Instead we prayed, an option suggested by the discovery that I did not have a confirmed onward flight. An hour later I was handed a boarding card as if nothing had happened, which in one sense it hadn't. Soon we were touching down at dawn, landing for the first time in Pakistan, and feeling so proud of ourselves because we were travelling hand baggage only. How far we had come. When we filmed

Broken Image in the Philippines the team had thirty-six items of luggage. Now we were going to make a video in Kabul, capital of Afghanistan, just carrying hand luggage.

But first we had to get to Kabul. It was, after all, a city under siege in a country racked by civil war, and not reachable by scheduled airline. The plan was to use the UN carrier, which flew reasonably regularly from Islamabad and sometimes had seats available, although at a price which had earned it the reputation as the most expensive airline in the world. We arrived in Islamabad on a Sunday, but the UN obviously had decided to stick with its Christian origins and not fly on Sundays. We established that the Monday flight was full, and then set off by taxi to find Rawalpindi, armed only with Terry's copy of the *Rough Guide to Pakistan*.

Islamabad is the modern capital city built not far from the ancient Rawalpindi; the road that links them offers a wonderful, constantly changing gallery of Pakistan's most exciting art form, the decorated truck. The blazing colours, the bold designs and slogans, the interesting metal attachments – they can take your mind off the driving. Rawalpindi was full of bustle, and the most intriguing thing was that we wandered through the street markets almost completely unregarded, no one demanding money or business. We found the *Rough Guide's* recommended restaurant, decided to bear with local culture and not sit in the women only section, and enjoyed an excellent meal, unencumbered by any idea of what it was.

The next morning the UN office assured us, several times, that we had got lucky, and seats were now available. Our reading of the local English language paper, which carried horribly graphic accounts of the results of a shell that had landed in a market place in Kabul, suggested that 'lucky' might not be the most suitable word. When we discovered that the previously full plane now had only one other passenger, our suspicions on this point were roused further. But then there were only nine seats, so perhaps we were getting paranoid.

After an hour's flight, interrupted only by the co-pilot distributing the in-flight catering – a Cadbury's chocolate eclair – we descended through the clouds to a breathtaking sight, a military base lined with Russian transport planes. Just to encourage us, we disembarked to be replaced by a CNN video crew, whose mountain of equipment and luggage challenged the pilot of the plane rather more than our hand baggage had done. How virtuous we felt.

A UN vehicle took us to Kabul, a forty-five minute drive that began by crossing a barren plateau surrounded by the mountains, and ended with passing an industrial area clearly left shattered and derelict by shell-fire, then row upon row of bleak concrete tenement blocks. All the way the man in charge was on his walkie-talkie, reporting our position. We were entering a war zone.

Tearfund had sent a relief team to work alongside a partner made up of expatriates working for the health and development of the Afghan people, many of whom had stayed through the Russian occupation and on into the civil war period. We were dropped at their office, then taken to the guest house; both were surrounded by sandbags up to the height of the ground-floor windows. I heard with interest the story of the hit on the room where I was sleeping, only slightly reassured that it had been empty at the time. We could hear the dull thump of shell-fire in the distance.

Tony Bird of the Tearfund team collected us and took us round to their house, where we met up with the other two members, Nic Parham and Alastair McDonald. We began to plan our short visit, which revealed the pressures of running a relief project in a remote and dangerous and Islamic location. The problem exercising their minds that evening was the tension over working with the local community leaders, the *waqils*, who were insisting that they should have some say as to who got food. I was glad that my only worry was whether we would be able to get a flight out again.

At that point the evening began to slip into a more surreal phase, as we went round for dinner to the UN club, which was populated by representatives of various nations who had decided for diverse reasons that Kabul was the place to be. Stephanie was the life and soul of the party; the rumour was that she was Cory Aquino's sister. The television in the corner was showing an episode of *Inspector Frost*. We walked back from this curious Western enclave through deserted unlit streets, with just an occasional glimmer of car headlights breaking the pre-curfew darkness. The cold night sky was ablaze with stars, which included a long, indistinct, cloud-like streamer stretched above us. Terry had been mixing with Jodrell Bank scientists just before he left, and proudly informed us that this was a grade one sighting of the comet Hyakutake.

The next morning we started at the warehouse where the grain and cooking oil were stored. The doors were unlocked; four rickety but elaborately decorated trucks roared into position, followed by another four, and in no time at all Nic had organised the loading of 80 tonnes. Afghans clambered high on to the massive pile of sacks, and with surprising ease hoisted, shifted and deposited the 100 kilo sacks of wheat into the back of the lorries. It was dark, it was dusty, it was full of diesel fumes, then it was done.

There was quite a story to these relief supplies. The team had arrived to ensure food was distributed through the fierce cold of the Afghan winter, when the temperature can fall to $-20°$ C. At that point the grain, a gift from the Canadian Foodgrain Bank, was still in Pakistan and there seemed no prospect of moving it. Urgent prayer had been called for back in the UK, and quite unexpectedly, the World Food Programme agreed to swap their food, already in Kabul, for the supplies stranded in Pakistan. Two days later, the warehouse in Pakistan caught fire, and the stocks were destroyed. Meanwhile the Tearfund team were beginning to organise the distribution of 1,350 tonnes of wheat, 65 tonnes of oil and 110 tonnes of lentils.

The need was great. The supply line into Kabul had been cut by one of the *mujaheddin* factions, and prices had begun to soar. The team had been told of people selling their blood for transfusions in order to buy food. Their problem was how to identify the most needy. Some were supplied through a mother and child health clinic; widows, disabled people and their families were given priority. Much of the supplies had been used to fund food-for-work schemes, which contributed to the rebuilding of the city and paid wages in the most valuable and appreciated currency – food.

So we followed the lorries up to the headquarters of Habitat, the UN agency organising the food for work schemes, where payment was to be made that afternoon. While Terry was recording the sacks being unloaded and positioned ready for distribution, there was suddenly a deafening explosion. I jumped what seemed to be several feet in the air. The video shows by its camera wobble that Terry also jumped; the soundtrack records the explosion – and the laughter that followed. They all knew that there was a gun emplacement just down the road, and they all knew the difference between outgoing and in-coming fire. We did not. We jumped. We were glad they thought it so funny.

That afternoon we saw the effects of war. It was not quite so funny. We were in the third of the city that had been reduced to little more than rubble. I thought back to the newsreels of Germany in 1945 from my days as a history teacher, and realised the pictures are always only a shadow of the reality. Some walls still stood, pockmarked by bullets, with holes punched through by tank-fire. Other buildings seemed to have dissolved into sand.

People still walked down the streets. There were even little fruit barrows among the ruins. Three hundred thousand people were surviving with no electricity or mainline water supply – quite how, I had no idea. Most extraordinary of all were the hillsides up beyond the wreckage, covered with sandy-coloured earth huts that from a distance looked like troglodyte dwellings. Behind them, the snow-capped mountains.

We met Ahmed on one of the food-for-work schemes. He was working with a group building a stone-lined drainage ditch designed to improve sanitation and help prevent flooding when the snow melted. He was twenty-six, his household of nine included his brothers and his two children. He came to the office in the afternoon, accompanied by three friends and their hand-cart. He had been working for two weeks, and the agreed rate was seven kilos of grain a day – a sack every two weeks. Ahmed assured me through our interpreter that this would feed his family for two weeks – although to get the grain milled into flour he would have to use one week's wages.

He loaded his hand-cart and they set off through the canyons of dereliction. They walked on steadily, impassive, ignoring Terry's efforts to grab the pictures. This involved him attempting to run to get ahead of them, trying to find an angle that did not have me or our vehicle in the background, then walking backwards while he held the camcorder to his eye. It was a virtuoso performance in an extraordinary setting.

There was another food-for-work scheme operating on the banks of the Kabul river, constructing flood defences. Dozens of men were working hard, digging out the bank, or filling the wire mesh coffers with stone, or manoeuvring them into position. Muslim men earning their crust courtesy of a combination of Western governments, the United Nations and a charity supported with money and prayer from people in churches across Britain and

Ireland: it was certainly a dimension of life beyond the news headlines.

We saw a little more of Kabul. We were stopped by a group of well-armed *mujaheddin* at one point, who were definitely not keen on the video camera they had seen being pointed out of the vehicle. There were a few minutes of anxious talking before they waved us on. We saw a newly installed hand-pump providing fresh water which the team was very proud of; we saw different areas of varying devastation. We saw the blossom beginning to come out on the trees. We saw women, only some covered completely in the anonymity of their *burqa*. The Taliban were the group outside firing in; they were yet to arrive and begin their own version of liberation, which would see women effectively removed from any participation in life in public. We noted the common sight of men lacking one or both legs, the dreadful legacy of landmines.

That evening there was a dinner party behind the sandbags at the Tearfund house. There was Tania from Oxfam, Cindy, Sophie from Norway. I noted that the three men organising a half-million-pound relief programme also seemed to be able to organise their social life quite well. It was a pleasant evening. Stephanie proudly supplied a bottle, an apple pie was duly appreciated, and I took the opportunity to send an e-mail via satellite phone to Colin, a fellow-elder at Teddington Baptist Church.

There were seats on the plane. We thought we had better take them. We had been in Kabul for less than three days, but we had gathered what we needed. The flight back was another of those Graham Greene moments. The hand-luggage-only Englishmen were joined by the Oxfam country director, an envoy who had been involved in peace negotiations, a middle-aged Irish UN soldier, and the head of the landmine clearance programme.

The Irishman wore his blue beret proudly, and discussed at great length the relative merits of living in Lebanon, the Congo and Kabul. The advantage of Lebanon, apparently, was that his wife felt able to visit him there. The landmine man reflected on the challenge created by ten million landmines. The statistics were chilling: 500,000 men, women and children had already been killed or maimed; every day there were 25 new victims. Ironically, the government had pressed him to clear the mines around the electricity pylons, so they could effect repairs and restore power: then they wanted him to put the mines back. Terry and I made a note to include in our video the cinema advertisement for the UK Working Group on Landmines, of which Tearfund was a member. Afghanistan was not the only country where Tearfund's partners were sometimes literally having to pick up the pieces of a form of warfare that could not distinguish combatants from non-combatants and which could not recognise a cease-fire.

We had a Friday to spare in Islamabad. It was, of course, the weekly holiday, and we strolled down the streets, with crowds of boys and young men playing cricket in the warm sunshine wherever there was an open space. In the evening we decided the local Afghan barbecue restaurant was the sensible option. It was all very pleasant, the relaxed atmosphere in stark contrast with the city just an hour away by plane. And there was live cricket on the television. Cricket in the hotel, cricket in the restaurant of the airport lounge in Karachi; it made the tortuous route home almost bearable.

After several landings in Pakistan, including a town I had never heard of where armed soldiers came and guarded the plane while passengers got off and on, we arrived in Bombay to transfer to the British Airways flight back to Heathrow. It landed on time at 6.30 a.m., so I was able to take the Palm Sunday Scout parade service at Teddington Baptist Church as planned. I confess: I milked the moment for all it was worth. Taking a church service immediately after twenty-four hours of non-stop travel returning from a hand-baggage-only trip to Afghanistan is the nearest I

will ever get to heroics. It's not much compared to those who opt
to go and work there, I know. It's nothing compared to those who
survive in a shell-shattered city.

21

On The Road Again

Who has not felt how sadly sweet
The dream of home, the dream of home?
Thomas Moore

My role was being changed, so for the last time I was discussing with colleagues the annual harvest challenge: how could we come up with resource materials for churches that would help them to celebrate their harvest festival joyfully, biblically and rooted in the real world? The year before, the material had focused on the mega-issues of food in the context of trade and oppression. So we decided on this occasion we should balance the approach and concentrate on telling a story – and perhaps we could find a way of weaving a Bible story together with a story from one of our partners, and thus emphasise the relevance of both.

So we did some praying and thinking through various Bible stories, and suddenly realised that while Andrew Lloyd Webber had elevated his amazing technicolour dreamcoat to world-wide stardom, there was more to the life of Joseph. He had predicted and then faced a major harvest challenge – the first world-wide food relief programme. I wrote off to partners in West Africa who were involved in agricultural work, and explained that we were looking to be able to video their work, and if their staff had any reflections or thoughts on this Bible story, that would be a great help. The first answer came by e-mail from Guinea. They would be pleased to host us, and we might be interested to know the name of the man in charge of the agricultural work: Joseph.

We duly arrived in Conakry, the capital city. In fact our arrival was the one really awkward moment of the entire visit. There were only the three of us: me, Richard the staff photographer and Terry the one-man video crew. We were whisked through the small and chaotic arrivals shed by a man who gave every impression of knowing who we were, and every impression that he was looking after us. When we emerged the other side, we discovered that he was expecting us to look after him. We looked round hopefully for our host, but there was no sign of anyone remotely interested in rescuing us from this man whose helpfulness was rapidly becoming threatening. As the planeload of passengers gradually dispersed, the other members of the helpful brigade who obviously met every plane were inevitably drawn to the only activity left – the three mean arrivals with nowhere to go.

Eventually, better late than never, the US cavalry appeared over the hill. David Carter certainly looked the part, his stetson, cowboy boots and accent allowing even the worst pupils of Sherlock Holmes to deduce he might have American origins. But he also had fluent French, and talked our way out past our helper and into a vehicle. Over the next few days we were to get to know him, and his vehicle, pretty well. David was the young man in charge of the work of CAMA Services in Guinea, the relief and development arm of the mission I had first met on that initial trip to Hong Kong. The majority of his life had been spent in West Africa, and we sensed his enjoyment at being the enthusiastic host sharing his local knowledge . . . and his country music.

The work was up-country. We had looked on a map and it was, well, three or four inches at least. But David assured us it was a good road, most of the way, and after all, he travelled it all the time. Dotted along the road were the homes of various Alliance missionaries, so we found ourselves on a holy version of a pub crawl, the main difference being the softness of the drinks and the distance between them. At each port of call David would have post to deliver, boxes to take on or unload. The boxes often seemed to involve animals. The outward journey was enlivened by a puppy, whose plaintive whining noises and box-destroying antics were only surpassed by the kittens with whom we shared the return trip.

Guinea is a long, narrow country, and we had to get from one end to the other. David was an enthusiastic driver, with only the very slightest hint of an ancestral link with a family of kamikaze pilots. He was unstinting of himself over the whole journey, as we covered about 700 miles in fifteen hours of driving over two days. He was unstinting with his country music, too, but willing to take as well as to give – U2 came across particularly well as West African jungle trail accompaniment.

The road was indeed good, most of the way. In fact a Brazilian contractor was turning it into a motorway, which made for some interesting variations. One moment we would be negotiating a busy African village main street, then descending a hillside on a winding red-dirt road, only shortly afterwards to be belting down a brand new two-lane shining tarmac highway. Occasionally they were almost tangled together, it being slightly unclear whether the motorway was actually open; we would be twisting round the dirt road which was itself criss crossing virgin tarmac. David explained that the problem with setting off down the tarmac at full speed was the possibility that you might arrive unannounced at a bridge only slightly, but significantly, incomplete.

It made for a varied journey. At night we saw the Hale-Bopp comet in the clear night sky, by day, we turned down the snake offered for sale by some children, in a peculiarly African version of the what-every-traveller-may-not-need stock range of the average motorway service station gift shop; we admired David's display of bravura confidence as he ignored the queue of traffic waiting for the antique ferry to cross the Niger river and drove on to the approach to the bridge, waving nonchalantly to the guard manning the barrier presumably intended to block access – David knew this bridge was complete, even if the road was as yet not opened to traffic; we survived the minor accident when a contractor's lorry lurched round a tight bend and clipped the wing of our vehicle, provoking a lengthy and animated discussion of tyre-tracks and braking speeds. And the country music played on.

We eventually arrived. We met Joseph. We quickly discovered that our journey was hardly traumatic in comparison with his own and those of his fellow-refugees, all 600,000 of them. Guinea borders Sierra Leone and Liberia; in both countries civil war, mindless violence and unspeakable atrocities had prompted this massive exodus. Women raped, their husbands cut up and sold as meat in the market-place – it was hard to hear and hard to believe. In one refugee camp we met six-year-old twins who had not spoken for two years since they had seen their parents murdered: their silence spoke volumes.

Joseph Knight was a large man in his forties, friendly, with a gently dignified manner. He had been a senior agricultural official in Liberia, a veteran of training courses in Italy, Japan and Germany. When rebel forces arrived in his home town in 1990 his wife had urged him to flee; his initial reluctance was overcome when his car had been commandeered and he had been forced to drive it at gunpoint. He and his family had walked the short distance to the river border, crossed it by canoe, then made a temporary and uncomfortable home in a kitchen outhouse nearby. 'We didn't want to come too far into Guinea,' he told me, 'because we didn't think the war was going to last long.'

It was not a very healthy environment, however, and his family became very sick. So he moved on to a nearby town, and discovered a church that welcomed them, and ensured they had food and clothing. It wasn't long before the church was asking his help to formulate a request for support for an agricultural project – he had never heard of Tearfund at that point, but when the church received its support, they asked Joseph to take on and run the project. Now he had become the regional agricultural supervisor for SECADOS, the African-run relief arm of the Evangelical Protestant Church of Guinea that had been established by CAMA. The projects he was responsible for were described by the Tearfund consultant as the best he had ever seen.

Their aim was to provide food for thousands of refugees. The parallels between Joseph in Egypt and Joseph in Guinea were remarkable. Both were exiles from their own country. Both had suffered greatly, and then been given great responsibility. Both had to face a harvest challenge in a foreign country. Both helped to feed their own countrymen. And both put their trust in the living God.

Joseph took us on a tour of his work, punctuated by welcomes from the local groups of SECADOS, which delighted in the name of *antennas*. They looked after us well, and we began to understand not only the detail of the agriculture, but also the dynamic of the whole project, its impact on the church and the refugees. The border areas had been flooded with refugees. In one province, we were told, they outnumbered the Guineans by four to one. Guinea, a predominantly Muslim nation, decided to welcome the visitors as helpfully as possible. The small Evangelical Church saw this as a new opportunity for service and witness: Emmanuel Kourouma, National Co-ordinator for SECADOS, told me, 'Before you tell somebody that you have faith you have to show it through your actions.'

CAMA Services had made significant efforts to equip the African leaders to take the opportunity. CAMA Services/ SECADOS had become one of the main agents for the UNHCR (United Nations) programme for delivering relief supplies to the refugee camps. Everywhere we went Muslim local government officials told us what a great job the church was doing; policemen saluted the church vehicles as they went past. But Guinea had refused to insist that all refugees stayed in camps; the need for ongoing food supplies was created both by decreasing supplies in the camps and the additional numbers of people living in the border towns and villages.

We discovered just how acute the problem was in the camps when we attended a food distribution in Nongoa camp. Most of the people were from Sierra Leone, and had been here for six years. Sakilah Falah told us he was eighty; his home was not far away, just the other side of the border. But he had lost three houses, a coffee and cocoa farm, and all his belongings. He was one of the group defined as 'vulnerables' – the old, blind and other handicapped people, unaccompanied children, pregnant and nursing mothers, chronic sick – who made up 30 per cent of the camp.

Joseph Kamba of SECADOS organised the distribution with tremendous energy and humour, a stocky man wearing a battered trilby that gave him the air of a West African Blues Brother as he dashed from place to place checking all was in order. Women in astonishingly colourful dresses sat in orderly rows as sacks of cornmeal were first piled up in front of them, and then, after a woman had stood to pray and say grace, each sack was distributed to a group of nine to be broken down further.

Then the problems began to emerge. The ration looked small enough; it was intended to last a month, but was having to stretch to three. Worse, the UNHCR had decided by decree rather than observation that there were only 20 per cent of the camp who were 'vulnerables', and only 'vulnerables' would get food. To make things more difficult, the cornmeal sacks marked 'Canadian Foodgrains Bank: A Christian Response to Hunger' were not that welcome to people whose staple diet was rice. Sakilah was mixing it with cassava leaves to make a not very appetising meal. Others were taking their ration down to the local market to exchange it for rice, even though supply and demand was making cornmeal a

222

cheap sell and rice an expensive purchase.

While Joseph Kamba did his stuff, Joseph Knight was being questioned hard by young men who were demanding to know how the 'non-vulnerables' in the camp were supposed to eat with the rations so small and the proportion of beneficiaries so low. It was the point at which one could see the vulnerability of the church forced by circumstances out of their control to deliver a bad deal. But at least Joseph could point to the schemes he was running, designed to help refugees outside the camps to grow their own food.

His expertise was in 'swamp' farming. The swamp was in fact a paddy-field, and rice was the main crop. SECADOS, with Tearfund's help, was helping refugees to buy or rent swamps; Joseph was helping them to make the most of them. Two rice crops could be obtained in the wet season and a further crop such as peanuts or sweetcorn could be grown in the dry season. He showed us a variety of crops being grown in swamps in a variety of settings, close to the town or deep in the jungle.

One swamp was being dug out to build a demonstration fish farm: there were large numbers engaged in serious digging activity in the heat, their legs submerged in mud as they discharged shovels at the banks. Richard's search for the action photo put him in the shovels' firing-line, much to everyone's amusement. Joseph also took us into the tropical forest to see a reforestation programme that was attempting to repair the damage created by the insatiable demand for firewood and timber when the nearby camp had been built.

Trees had also been planted in the camp itself. The logic was simple: they would provide some shade now, and they would be there when the camp was gone. We followed Joseph round the camp, attracting a larger and larger crowd of following children. Once again I could do my famous Pied Piper impression, and our counting chants resulted in a sea of smiling faces. Richard, always a more spiritual being, got them sharing choruses with him.

Meanwhile the elected leader of the camp was telling me of the terrors of the past and the realities of the present: 'There is hunger in this camp,' he told me.

On Sunday morning we asked if we could worship with the refugees. In fact, at a nearby camp called Fandou Yema, there was a church that was combined, local Guineans and refugees worshipping together, despite their language barrier – the refugees from Sierra Leone and Liberia share English as a common language, the Guineans French. We walked between the simple mud huts with the blue polythene roof-sheets, watching children playing and gathering water from the well, while mothers cooked ready for Sunday lunch – our Sunday lunch, as it turned out.

The leaders of the camp showed me their school, and explained that this camp of around five hundred families from both Sierra Leone and Liberia had come together because they were Christians. 'We built a shelter for worship first, before we built our homes,' one of them said. That day there were around two hundred adults and two hundred children gathered for worship. Various choirs came and sang for us, including a choir of little children whose tiny conductor got very exasperated with them. The drums beat, the feet shuffled in rhythm.

Then it was my turn. I had attempted my usual resistance, still conscious that they probably had more to teach me about following Christ than I them; but I had been persuaded. I was introduced with an instruction to mothers to breast-feed their children to keep them quiet during the sermon. I could think of a few churches in Britain where such an instruction would have been useful, if not culturally acceptable. When I mentioned that Jesus could understand their situation because he too had been a refugee, there was a loudly audible response of agreement; this meant a lot to them.

After the service the pastors invited us to join them in a little room at the back of the church building. They had two requests, two messages they wanted us to take back to Christians in Britain and Ireland. The first was for prayer: prayer for peace in Liberia and Sierra Leone, and prayer for the church in Guinea, that its witness would be strong, that people might know 'the peace of mind that comes from God, which means more than a plate of food'. The second was to ask people to receive a verse, Psalm 41:1, as a promise from God: *'Blessed are those who have regard for the weak'* (NIV Inclusive edition).

That morning I caught a glimpse of the agony of the refugee experience. One pastor had said to me, 'We are tired and we want to go home.' But then home was also where memories of pain would be renewed. Another woman had said 'We know we have to go home, but we don't know what happened to our husbands and children. We will go back when we know they are safe and we can be reunited.'

There was something more than agony, however. The Jesus who could empathise with their flight from violence into a foreign land was the Jesus they had worshipped with such enthusiasm. Outside the church a woman tugged my sleeve and pointed to the horizon where, no more than a couple of miles away, there was a ridge of hills sharply etched against the searing blue of the sky. A solitary tree stood out on the skyline. 'That tree,' she said, 'that's home.' Just across the border, every day in view, a tree that was a reminder of how near and how far it was.

The joy in that church in Fandou Yema is a reminder to me that there is hope. Hope that exists because of another tree on a hill. Across the world that tree has become the symbol of hope in the face of despair, triumph in the midst of tragedy. That tree is an empty cross because suffering did not and does not have the last word. My travels have taken me to teeming cities and remote communities, and whatever the pain, the injustice and the apparently insuperable odds, I have discovered that the resurrection life of the kingdom of God breaks out in the lives of ordinary people, people who may seem of no value in the world's judgment, but who are worth everything to the one who made them. And one day, when all the travelling is done, I will have the privilege of meeting them again.

Postscript

It was just another Saturday morning in Twickenham when the phone rang. Helen, my younger daughter, answered it. 'It's Graham Kendrick here,' the voice said, 'could I speak to your dad?' That was how I first heard the song I had commissioned Graham to write for Tearfund's twenty-fifth anniversary. While Helen was trying to explain to a friend that Graham Kendrick was famous – well, sort of, because the friend had never heard of him – I was listening to a curious kind of first performance. The line was quite good, but it hardly did the song justice, even though I doubt Graham would claim that his songs are best heard as an unaccompanied solo down a telephone line with the washing machine hard at work in the background.

The song encapsulated the work of Tearfund, drawing together the full breadth of interest and impact of the work of its partners around the world and beautifully capturing the challenge that has been at the heart of Tearfund's communication ever since it began. I have been deeply privileged both to have witnessed the dedicated commitment of partners, and to a tiny extent entered into the experience of the poor they serve, and also to have had the opportunity to follow my own calling and share in the communication process.

Every time I have begun to enter into the reality of the life of the poor, its joys and its suffering, I have done so in the context of being with those who are deeply involved in making a difference, and knowing that I could help to make a difference by coming home and telling others. I have often summarised the communication task as explaining the reality of the Third World, presenting the relevance and challenge of the Bible to that reality and introducing Tearfund as a channel of response. My involvement in that task has resulted in a personal enrichment the Croydon schoolteacher never imagined possible. I have discovered and preached that even when we feel overwhelmed by the needs of the world, we are simply but profoundly and persistently called to do what we can.

At the same time I have often faced the same problem with Tearfund that Helen found that Saturday morning. Being well-known in some churches is only fame of a kind: Tearfund may be the twelfth largest charity in Britain in terms of voluntary donations; it may have an income of over £24 million pounds a year and send its magazine out to over 120,000 people. But millions of people have never heard of it. Tearfund is famous; well, sort of.

If this book is your first introduction to Tearfund, or even if it isn't, I will end it with Graham Kendrick's words to act as a summary. But first I will do my job and make sure that you know the address and telephone number just in case you have been inspired or encouraged enough to want to know more, or to send a donation:

Tearfund, 100 Church Road, Teddington TW11 8QE telephone: 0845 355 8355. Or you can e-mail *enquiry@tearfund.dircon.co.uk*

But don't miss out on the reality of the words I first heard down the phone that Saturday morning.

> *Beauty for brokenness*
> *hope for despair*
> *Lord, in your suffering world*
> *this is our prayer.*
> *Bread for the children,*

justice, joy, peace,
sunrise to sunset
your Kingdom increase.

Shelter for fragile lives,
cures for their ills,
work for the craftsmen,
trade for their skills.
Land for the dispossessed,
rights for the weak,
voices to plead the cause
of those who can't speak.

Refuge from cruel wars,
havens from fear,
cities for sanctuary,
freedoms to share.
Peace to the killing fields,
scorched earth to green,
Christ for the bitterness,
his cross for the pain.

Rest for the ravaged earth,
oceans and streams,
plundered and poisoned,
our future, our dreams.
Lord, end our madness,
carelessness, greed;
make us content
with the things that we need.

Lighten our darkness,
breathe on this flame
until your justice burns

brightly again;
until the nations
learn of your ways,
seek your salvation
and bring you their praise.

God of the poor,
friend of the weak,
give us compassion we pray.
Melt our cold hearts,
let tears fall like rain,
come change our love
from a spark to a flame.